PHILOSOPHY FOR CREATIVE LEADERSHIP

*How philosophy can turn people into
more effective leaders*

PHILOSOPHY FOR CREATIVE LEADERSHIP

How philosophy can turn people into more effective leaders

Pierre Casse & Paul George Claudel

ATHENA PRESS
LONDON

PHILOSOPHY FOR CREATIVE LEADERSHIP
How philosophy can turn people into more effective leaders
Copyright © Pierre Casse, Paul George Claudel 2007

ISBN 10-digit: 1 84401 920 9
ISBN 13-digit: 978 1 84401 920 5

First Published 2007 by
ATHENA PRESS
Queen's House, 2 Holly Road
Twickenham TW1 4EG
United Kingdom

Printed for Athena Press

Contents

PART III: THE PTL JOURNAL

Man is the measure of all things.

Protagoras (485–411 BC)

Part I

A philosophical model

Before you start reading...

How do you like the idea of a quiz right at the beginning of the book?

Very good! So here's a little quiz that will basically tell you if you should (or should not) read this book. After all why should you spend your time (precious, according to this book) reading something which has absolutely no meaning or interest for you?

The following set of easy questions will tell you if there is indeed something useful in the following chapters – useful for you, that is. So, here we go:

1. Are you in any way concerned by the orientation of your life and what's happening to you? (Y/N)

2. Do you care about better understanding who you are and why? (Y/N)

3. Do you sometimes wonder why you think, feel and behave the way you do? (Y/N)

4. Are you interested in reviewing where you stand vis-à-vis your life? (Y/N)

5. Do you wonder where you are coming from and where you are going as a human being? (Y/N)

6. Do you want to explore practical ways to improve the quality of your personal decisions? (Y/N)

7. Do you sometimes wonder why people around you do what they do? (Y/N)

8. Is knowing the difference between right and wrong an important issue for you? (Y/N)

9. Would you like to know more about your talents and personal resources? (Y/N)

10. Are there things in your life that bother you? (Y/N)

11. Are you willing to challenge your basic assumptions about your life? (Y/N)

12. Does philosophy, and its purpose, intrigue you? (Y/N)

13. Do you believe in the power of emotions? (Y/N)

14. Do you understand your own feelings? (Y/N)

15. Are you eager to own your life? (Y/N)

16. Do you wonder why some people commit suicide? (Y/N)

17. Do you think that your professional life could be more meaningful? (Y/N)

18. Is entertainment important for you? (Y/N)

19. Do you care about others' lives? (Y/N)

20. Do you agree that knowledge is better than ignorance?

Debriefing following the quiz (should you read this book?):

If you have answered 'Yes' to more than twelve of the above questions, there is a good chance that you will find the book interesting and in line with some of your key expectations. You should read it, challenge it and enjoy it. Build your own book around this one. You can do it. It will be the 'book of your life'. Part III of the book will help you in this endeavour.

If you have answered 'Yes' to between six and eleven of the questions, you may be reluctant to embark on a journey of self-examination. This could be because you do not think that the topic (you and your life) is relevant, or because you believe that you already have the answers. Fair enough. Our advice is to take a look at the book. Perhaps there's a chance that you will find some of it stimulating and useful. Just try. At least go through the testing section.

If you have answered 'Yes' to only between one and five of the questions, we do not believe that this book is for you. Skip it. Ignore it. That's fine.

So, you decide!

Introduction: Why link philosophy and leadership?

Here we go...

This book is about the fundamental meaning of life (yours and mine) and how the fact of being able to identify this meaning can lead to a more purposeful, happy existence, and have a better interface with other people as a leader.

Since the search for the meaning of the world in general and of life in particular has always been the field of philosophy, this book is in its own way a book of philosophy.

But unlike many books of philosophy, its aim is essentially practical and related to two essential questions, i.e.:

1. How can a philosophical grasp of the world (including our own way of looking at it) actually help us to understand the deeper purpose of our lives?

2. And how can we effectively make use of our understanding to focus our actions and indeed *live a better life and become more effective leaders*?

These are the two main questions that this book will pose and attempt to answer. It is constructed around a model which claims to be a representation of life as we experience it. The model is very simple in the way that it pictures the structure of life in its most essential elements. The model is called the **Project-to-Live,** or the **PTL** for short.

The PTL model is structured around a cluster of basic enquiries that we all go through at one point or another in our lives:

> Cluster 1: What is the meaning of my life? What makes me tick? Is there an ultimate meaning to my existence on this planet?

> Cluster 2: What are my personal strengths/weaknesses (capabilities) and aspirations (wants), and how are they different from other people's?
>
> Cluster 3: Am I doing the right thing? Are my actions in line with my fundamental aspirations? How should I relate to other people? Why are they important?
>
> Cluster 4: What are my feelings and emotions? What are they telling me? Am I listening to them? How can I use them in a more effective and meaningful way?
>
> Cluster 5: Am I really responsible for my own life? Am I free? Do I own my life?

By answering the above questions (and more in the text), we will learn to understand why we do what we do and feel what we feel. We'll also hopefully draw from this the lessons that will allow us to live better, i.e. more in accordance with the ultimate purpose of our life.

Obviously it would be presumptuous of us to overlook the two following qualifications to what we have just said:

First, that the aim is to improve our condition and not to live a perfect life, where everything would be under our absolute and omniscient control, a hypothesis which would be absurd, given the immense amount of factors impacting on our existence that we cannot grasp or master.

Second, that the improvements we are entitled to aspire to are of a personal nature. We do not intend to offer a universal code of behaviour that we would claim is superior to whatever ethical codes may already exist, but only a series of *guidelines* based on an overall understanding of the meaning of our life in general. These guidelines can be adapted to your personal situation, and we believe they can help you manage your life in a way that should lead to your greater satisfaction.

The book has three main parts:

PART 1. THE MODEL

A description of what the philosophical model (the Project-to-Live) is about and what it can mean for each of us. The way by which we will proceed is to expose the PTL model progressively by looking at its different key components in succession and answering the key questions previously outlined.

PART 2. TESTS AND SELF-ASSESSMENT EXERCISES

We will offer a series of selected instruments that can give a chance to you, the reader, to take stock of some of your strengths and weaknesses from a philosophical (PTL) viewpoint. It is made up of five personal assessments and exercises which will result in increasing your awareness about what you are and enhancing your skills in managing the different facets of your capacity to live.

PART 3. A JOURNAL

This is a working tool that we invite the reader to use to make the model alive and really useful. It is a step-by-step approach to applying the PTL model, learning and improving our lives.

Each chapter will be presented around four questions:

- What is it? (Definition of the topic to be covered)
- What does it mean for me? (Personal implications)
- What is the red thread? (Structure of the text to be presented)
- What are the leadership implications of the model? (Leadership improvement)

We invite you (the reader) to go through the book with a pencil in hand and write down what you strongly agree on, deeply disagree with and/or simply do not understand. Our ultimate (and ambitious) goal is to trigger some meaningful thinking about what's happening in your life and what you can do about it to make it better. We also hope that you will enjoy putting your life into perspective. After all, it is your life!

Last, but not least, we have tried to create an *interactive book* so that the process of reading and reflecting is dynamic and involving. From time to time you will find questions and statements that will require (if you wish) some stopping and thinking on your part. These 'breakers' can also be used as topics for small group discussions. We hope that you will also enjoy the process.

But hang on a minute! What does all this have to do with leadership or becoming more effective leaders? Well, the writers' consideration is the following: leading is about *human beings leading other human beings*. Therefore the foundation of effective leadership has to be to understand how people function, what it is that makes us tick, what is behind everything that we do or feel. The more skilful we can become in grasping our motivations and behaviours first as leaders and others' as followers, the better chance we will have of inducing in our team members the conduct that we expect in order to obtain higher achievements.

So, even though we do provide a section called 'Leadership implications' at the end of each chapter, which points out how the key aspects of the philosophical model of life relate to leadership practices, the emphasis of this book will be on understanding what lies behind the behaviour of the person as an individual, rather than going through yet another repetition of what should be the right leadership 'tricks of the trade' in the classic sense.

All men and all women are philosophers. If they are not conscious of having philosophical problems, they have, at any rate, philosophical prejudices. Most of these theories which they take for granted, they have absorbed them from their intellectual environment or their tradition. Since few of these theories are consciously held, they are prejudices in the sense that they are held without critical examination, even though they may be of great importance for the practical actions of people, and for their whole life.

Karl Popper

1. What is philosophy, in a nutshell?

What is it?

In this chapter, we shall examine what philosophy is and what purpose it serves. We'll try to show that philosophy is indeed part of our day-to-day life. We shall demonstrate that we are all philosophers (one way or another) and that there is perhaps nothing more important than for us human beings to philosophise.

What's in it for me (the reader)?

This first chapter will help you review what philosophy can contribute to you. It will show that philosophy is not a simple and passive exercise but also a very active endeavour by which we all participate (yes, you too!) in the interpretation (creation?) of reality and the elaboration of knowledge. From this chapter, you can expect to get a better grasp of how philosophy, in general, can bring you to a better life.

What is the red thread?

The chapter will include the following questions and issues:

1. What is philosophy, or what are we talking about?
2. How do we build up our understanding of reality?
3. What is knowledge?
4. How does the mind of a philosopher work?
5. What does philosophy mean for me?

1. What is philosophy, or what are we talking about?

Philosophy is simply the instrument that we (human beings) use to examine the way we give *meaning* and *value* to the world in general and our lives in particular.

Please retain these two words:

- Meaning: What is the sense (or purpose) of... (whatever)?

- Value: How important is it for me, us and other human beings?

It can also be defined as a process by which we represent and understand the world. Some people will go so far as saying that it is a tool that we use to invent our reality and move forward with our individual and collective existences.

So philosophy indeed is a serious business. It is about us looking at ourselves and reflecting on how we relate to the environment that we live in (including other beings). It is about how we make sense of everything inside and outside our body.

To 'philosophise' is to be able to put things into perspective and try to understand what's happening to us by using our rational capability. It is a fundamental way of being human! It is a way for us human beings to survive and develop ourselves.

According to the above working definition, we are all philosophers because we are all concerned with fundamental questions such as:

- Why do I exist?

- What is real?

- Why do I die?

- What is the meaning of my life?

- What is the truth?

- Who is right and wrong?

- What is fair?

- Am I free?

- Why do I have to work so hard?

- What is justice?

- Other issues? (Many others...)

Question (to you, the reader)

Have you been asking those questions too? If yes, which one(s) in particular? If no, why not?

2. How do we build up our understanding of reality?

At every moment of our life, we form in our minds a picture, a representation of things, which we call our *idea* or our knowledge of the world. This idea or knowledge is composed of a multitude of concepts that are interconnected and constitutes a subjective and yet coherent way of defining our worlds (internal and external).

One can view the question of meaning as the very essence of our thinking. It can be expressed in the form of very simple questions such as: *'What is it?'* or *'What does it mean?'*

We ask this question about the sense of things every time we come across a new object and a new event, as well as when we look at a well-known situation from a different angle.

In some cases, the answers are already implanted in our brains and minds (we possess a set of ready-made answers to many questions we raise during a normal day). In many other situations, we must reflect on it and then decide on the proper interpretation of what the thing is.

We also question our usual ways of defining things because things constantly change and meanings become obsolete.

The main point is that we cannot live in a meaningless environment. So we invent our reality. Actually we can – in a way – go as far as saying that for us human beings nothing is real *per se*. It is all related to the constructions of our human minds. This observation raises a few important (and very old and still pending) 'philosophical' questions:

- If nothing is 'real' *per se*, how is it that we know what we know?

- Why do we produce the explanations of the world that we produce, and not others?

- Are there better ways to construct our reality, and if so how do we know that it is the case and how do we produce them?

- How do we invent our new interpretations of what is when we are still attached to our old ways?

- How do we know that what worked in the past is not effective any more?

- If nothing is absolute, how can we decide on the truth and on what's right and wrong?

- Was the human brain programmed to come up with the explanations of the world as it did throughout the evolution of the species?

The conclusion is that everybody gives meaning to what is. All human beings are, one way or another, concerned about what things (people, events and objects) mean to themselves and others. Nobody is indifferent in the face of all these questions. Philosophy is the art of questioning our ways of existing and interacting with the natural and social environments that we did not necessarily volunteer to be part of.

Question

Are you also concerned with the way you construct things in your own mind, and do you accept the idea that if nothing is real *per se*, then everything may be possible?

Your answer is:

3. What is knowledge?

Much is being said today about knowledge and how it goes far beyond the mere notions of facts or information. What this generally implies is that for knowledge to be useful, to have a value for us, it needs to have a *meaning*. Knowledge, therefore, is generally viewed in most current books and articles as *meaningful information*.

In this book, we would like to go a bit deeper in the definition of knowledge. We will try to describe how it is structured in our minds, so as to avoid confusion in the terms we use but also and more importantly in order to understand and take better advantage of the extraordinary richness of our mental constructions.

Actually, knowledge is basically our idea, our representation of the world. It is made of all the meanings that we attribute to what we perceive, with our mind and our body. Knowledge is the map we human beings use to guide our behaviour.

We can distinguish between three different categories of components that make up our knowledge and which differ according to the nature of the reference (more about the reference later) that they are built upon. These different categories of components are:

1. Data
2. Information
3. Wisdom

And to be complete and not leave out those who include in their idea of the world a belief in a supernatural life we shall add a fourth category that is:

4. Creed

(Creed, however, differs from the other three because it is based on an act of faith rather than on a rational deduction based on sense perceptions.)

We now propose to explore these different components of our knowledge and to indicate how they result in the structuring of our perception (construction) of the world into four corresponding fields or disciplines (maps) that we shall call **science, experience, philosophy** and **religion** (or **spirituality**). We shall also examine how the different components of our knowledge can contribute to the actual carrying out of our existence.

DATA

The first layer of our knowledge is formed of *data*, and the way we collect and organise it is called *science*.

In the scientific way of thinking, the meaning of things clearly lies *within* the domain that is being investigated (say, botany, psychology, physics or management), among the things (objects/people/events) that we aim to understand.

Each element of the domain under examination is defined in

relation to another element of the same domain, so that all these elements end up referring to one another in a tightly knit self-encompassing network of meaning.

In the scientific approach, each object/event of the domain, once it has been understood by reference to another already known element, can in turn become a reference of meaning for all the new things that we will subsequently attempt to understand and integrate in our knowledge.

Thus our scientific knowledge is built on a multitude of references of meaning, none of which plays any dominant role.

In addition, one can consider that all these references and the networks of meaning built through their interconnections are of an objective, self-contained nature.

They are not linked in any way to the purpose or the will of the observer (we who identify and build them).

In that sense we can qualify them as 'external' or 'neutral' (objective), as opposed to the 'internal (to us)' or 'intentional' (subjective) connections of meaning that form our other levels of knowledge, as we will see further down, and given this neutral character we shall designate this body of meanings simply as *data*.

It would take too long to describe here how data actually reach our minds, but let us only mention it is merely the result of our perceptions (the physical data detected by our senses) converted into *concepts* and then into so-called *facts*.

It is only when our perceptions are transformed into concepts that we can begin to process them mentally in order to organise our knowledge.

However, let's keep in mind that we must be very careful with the word 'data' because it can give us the impression that we can access the real world and what it is without filtering it through our brains and minds, which is obviously impossible. Everything for us human beings is in its very nature subjective and questionable.

We could also say that when data meet concepts then they become facts that are just *'verified' assumptions*! (Let's note here that a big debate among philosophers has been around what comes first, i.e. data or concepts. Do we observe first and get the concepts out of data or do we come up with hypotheses or concepts first and then check if the data confirms them or not?)

We like to think that science is built upon neutral observations that are independent of our personal intentions and makes it universal, objective and communicable.

Again, let's mention that it is also very important that this first and significant layer of knowledge also results from experimentation, so that we physically validate (verify) our hypotheses and/or conclusions. It seems that by so doing, we are active partners in the making of 'reality'.

The typical questions that science answers take the following forms: 'What is it? How does it work?' In other words, what are the causal or logical connections between the different elements that compose our world?

We must understand, however, that science is just a generic word to designate a form of knowledge that we all use constantly in our everyday lives. For indeed we all need to collect and store data in our personal files and in our memories, so that we can use it when necessary.

Data is the raw material out of which we build our understanding of the world. Even if it is 'meaningless' as such, it becomes, as we will see, meaningful once it is connected to our overall representation of the world and to our needs.

The value of our scientific knowledge therefore rests in its potential to be eventually exploited as a source of information and wisdom.

Question

Can you identify something that you can for sure define as a mere fact?

INFORMATION

The second layer of our knowledge is composed of *information* and the total of our information constitutes our *experience*.

We build our experience by linking the facts that form our scientific knowledge to the *intentions* that we develop as human/living beings.

By 'intentions', we mean any purpose, desire or will that motivates us as we carry on with our life. Our intentions are the immediate manifestation of our existence as living beings. They express our multitude of needs for comfort, for beauty, for food, for shelter, for love, for achievement and so on.

Every time that we connect a network of mere facts to such

an aspiration, we come up with a new piece of meaning that becomes usable for practical purposes.

We call such meaningful connections of facts to our intentions *information,* which etymologically signifies the impression of a form, an impact on us, as opposed to unrelated scientific data, which we have qualified as neutral, as having no effect whatsoever as such on our existence.

In other words, information tells us what the things we observe and have connected to one another through logical/causal links mean to us. By connecting the plain factual data of science to our intentions, we understand it in relation to our personal interests and ourselves.

This information that we gather as we carry out our existence we call our *experience,* in the sense that it results from the effect that the things we have encountered have actually had on our life.

Question
Can you single out a fact that is actually a piece of information?

WISDOM
The third layer of our knowledge is formed by our *wisdom* and we refer to it as *philosophy.*

Here we take a quite different approach from that which led to our scientific or to our experimental understanding of the world.

We start from the things that belong to the world and question them even further and further. The philosophical thinker ends up, through a succession of regressions, by taking one step back from the whole and by asking the question of the meaning of the world in general.

Thus the typical philosophical questions are: 'What is the meaning of the world?' or 'What is the purpose of my life?' or again, 'How does it all fit together?'

In order to understand the world or everything that is as a whole, we need to relate to a reference that, by definition, will lie *outside* it, so to speak.

This type of reference has been qualified as *transcendent,* since it is set from the start as being beyond the world in question. It is also interesting to point out that the kind of philosophy which attempts to give a meaning to the world in reference to such a transcending foundation is called *meta-physics*, which literally signifies a knowledge which reaches beyond the natural world.

The metaphysical reference is by definition the ultimate reference, the ultimate foundation of the meaning of the world and thus of our existence and of everything that these notions encompass.

As regards philosophy, therefore, as per its above definition, and unlike what happens with science or experience, the reference of meaning on which this aspect of our knowledge is based *is singular*. Everything converges towards this one and only foundation of sense, so that our knowledge of things becomes a unified network of meaning.

This type of knowledge, as it is all encompassing, is also referred to as *wisdom*. It is meant to provide an answer to all our questions (what things mean and what we should do), including the one of whether and why there may be some questions that cannot usefully be raised...

What remains to be determined, however, is whether we are speaking here of an *external* or *neutral* reference, as in science, unrelated to our personal purpose or will, or with an *internal* or *intentional* reference, as in experience, that provides meaning only in connection to our own will and desires.

We shall see below, as we go through a quick summary of the history of philosophical thinking, that in fact the ultimate reference of meaning has moved through time from a 'neutral' concept to an 'intentional' concept, embedded in our very being. It's a fascinating transformation!

Questions

What is your own definition of wisdom? Does it match the one mentioned just above?

CREED

Those who believe in a supernatural world can add their religious creed (or spiritual outlook) as a fourth layer to the structure of their knowledge. For such people, philosophy will then represent a complementary explanation of our existence in this world.

The comments that we made concerning wisdom or philoso-phy can simply be transferred here instead, except that the ultimate reference of meaning in this case will essentially be metaphysical and transcendent, be it God or any other form of supernatural entity or concept.

Most philosophers would argue that there is by nature an unbridgeable gap between this supernatural layer of knowledge and the other three that we mentioned before. They will state that wisdom is all built rationally and based on our experience, whilst a religious (or spiritual) understanding of the world can only emanate from a form of revelation adopted by virtue of an act of *faith* (some people even talk of a 'leap' of faith).

We do also realise that some readers may feel offended by the philosophical claim that the ultimate reference could lie in man himself, and that man can thus rid himself of the notion of God to give a meaning to the world and his own existence.

The purpose here however is not to exclude the possibility of God as the creator of all things. Our position is that, by definition, belief in God is a matter of faith and not of reason or philosophical knowledge. Our philosophical approach is to *rationally* explore the meaning of our existence and of the world in relation to the ultimate reference of meaning that we are actually able to *experience with our senses*. This, of course, does not preclude the possibility for anyone who believes in God to think that He created us with the expectation that we would use our reason to give meaning and purpose to our existence on earth.

In any case, it appears that what many philosophers have to say about the value of life and the way to live does not contradict but in fact to a large extent validates the highest ethical values that emanated from the religious foundation of the past (even though their way of reaching and validating such values may be different).

For those who do believe in transcendence and in God, their creed will, as we said earlier, constitute either a fourth 'metaphysical' level of their knowledge or simply replace the 'philosophical' level if they are satisfied with the dogmatic interpretation of life provided in the scriptures.

Question

What is your position regarding faith? How can it coexist with a 'philosophical' outlook on life and the world?

Let us stop here for a few minutes and reflect on the ideas just presented.

Examine the very structure of your knowledge:

1. What is your usual way of dealing with facts? (Pick one of the following or a position in between.)

   Facts are very important for me. I have a kind of scientific mind. I am highly pragmatic and down-to-earth. I am a realist.

   I am not very good at facts. I prefer to trust my impressions. I find facts cold and impersonal. I prefer to go with my intuition than with the so-called facts.

2. How do you manage information? (Pick one or a position in between.)

   I always relate things and people to me. I never stop looking for something meaningful in the situations that I am involved in. I love to learn new things as they affect me.

   I like to be an observer and watch what's happening to people (and even to myself). I like to think that I am objective and impartial. I am detached and cool.

3. How do you practise wisdom? (Pick one or a position in between.)

   I am concerned with the basic questions relating to my existence. I spend time analysing the meaning of what I think, feel and do. I accept metaphysics as an important way of understanding what we are and why.

   I perceive philosophy as an interesting but not very useful exercise. I do not like to speculate about life and other 'esoteric' issues. Either we know or we don't.

4. Do you value faith and believe in God? (Pick one or a position in between.)

   I am a religious person. I strongly believe that God is behind everything we are and do. God is the source of all meanings. I have faith and define myself as a spiritual being.

I am not a believer, and I think that to rely on faith to live one's own life is basically to abdicate ownership and responsibility. I see it as a sign of weakness.

4. How does the mind of a philosopher work?

'Philosophers' are always concerned about the meaning and value of everything. They keep probing what's happening inside and outside their own minds. They are curious and keep investigating not only what is but also how we make sense of objects, people and events. For them, nothing is definite and final.

Here are three examples of what they consider and examine in a systematic way:

1. Who am I as an interpreter of reality, and what can I know?

This is the fundamental question about our identity and the power that we have to decipher reality. It leads to the issue of what the position of mankind is in the world.

2. Why do I exist? Where do I come from and where am I going?

This question has been asked from the beginning of time. There is no guarantee that we will ever have an answer to it. Actually, there is a good chance that the question is irrelevant. We should still ask it, however.

3. Can I explain things differently and more meaningfully?

This is maybe the most practical question we can ask. If we live in a world defined and explained through the power of the human brain and mind, then it seems that we must learn how to continuously manage our subjective interpretations of what is so that we optimise the quality of our lives.

5. What does philosophy mean to me?

It means nothing if you are not interested in the deep, profound meaning of your life. It means everything if you are concerned about:

- Understanding yourself as a 'creator' of reality
- Getting a better grasp of what life is all about as well as the meaning of all your day-to-day activities
- Being in charge of your own life, and deciding on what it could/should mean
- Leading from the foundation of understanding the other person.

Let's summarise by asking two questions (please read them very carefully):

Question 1

(Once more) why is philosophy so important?

If the purpose of philosophy were only to attribute a meaning to the world or to our existence in general, whilst this would certainly be an intellectually stimulating exercise, it would probably not be of great value to us as human beings.

The real value of philosophy is to help us identify an ultimate yardstick of meaning (that we shall call 'reference' later on) to which we can use to relate to the world in general. Through the use of that yardstick, we are then in a position to refer any particular element of the world or any situation or event of our existence to this foundation in order to understand them, and to understand and stimulate the behaviours of others.

In other words, philosophy gives us a single, stable reference that provides a coherent answer to all our interrogations, a converging meaning for all the experiences of our lives, including of course everything that we do or feel in the course of our professional activity in business. That's why philosophy is so important for everybody!

Question 2

What is (again) the broader meaning of philosophy?

We have just explained that by the term philosophy we implied the field/layer of our knowledge which contained the understanding of the world as a whole and of our existence in general.

We should point out, however, that the notion of philosophy includes many meanings and has been used by thinkers throughout history to designate different areas of rational investigation. For instance, for some great philosophers philosophy essentially implied the understanding of the process of acquiring knowledge, in all its forms (the name for this branch of philosophy is *epistemology*).

In that sense, we could consider here that our entire description of what knowledge is, including all four of its fields/layers mentioned in this chapter, is in itself a philosophical exercise.

We shall in this book apply the word philosophy preferably to what Aristotle called the 'first' philosophy or 'metaphysics'. That is the study of the meaning of the world and of our lives in general as a path towards the understanding of everything that is and everything that we (and others) do or feel, in relation to an ultimate foundation of meaning.

Remember this: philosophy is about studying the meaning of the world and of our existence!

What are the leadership implications?

The question is: How can philosophy help somebody be a better leader, and even more how can it make a leader a better creative leader?

Powerful leaders are imaginative, flexible and result-oriented. Philosophy will help by providing the necessary tools to:

1. Create knowledge to explain and impact reality

2. Measure the impact of one's own behaviour on reality

3. Act upon what exists and make it evolve in the 'right' direction.

CREATE KNOWLEDGE

Leaders can control knowledge by managing the reference. Here are a few leadership guidelines to help do it effectively:

*   Know how each individual answers some basic questions, such as: Why do I work? What is the meaning of performing well? Why should I challenge myself at work? (Where am I coming from?)

*   Create a working environment that *stretches* in the sense that it gives people an opportunity to review and challenge their usual ways of understanding things and people. (How can people expand and grow?)

- Make sure that people share some basic references at the team level. Involve team members in the creation of the team vision. (What are we fighting for together?)

It has been shown that effective leaders are able to mobilise their partners around a joint and exciting reference. They also involve the people in the choice of the reference.

Creative leaders go one step further by encouraging people in the 'open source knowledge process' where everybody is invited to contribute to the elaboration of the new explanations of reality, i.e. new business models, emerging organisational behaviour, teamwork, motivation and even leadership.

MEASURE BEHAVIOUR

Creative leaders know that the significance of their behaviour is not in what they say or do but in other people's reactions. They are therefore extremely astute in watching how people understand them and respond to them. In other words they are capable of reinventing themselves according to the stimuli that they get from the environment they belong to.

ADAPT

Not only do creative leaders have a wide repertoire of ready-made answers to face many different situations, but they also have developed the capacity over time to invent new behaviours that will make them more successful. They are quite good at switching from one pattern to another, and if nothing works, to come up with a new approach to a given situation.

To sum up, one can say that philosophy can assist the creative leaders in:

1. Increasing their awareness of the relativity of all meanings.
2. Learning how to combine meanings (what is it?) and values (how important is it?) together.
3. Adapting their attitudes and behaviours to various situations.

There are no facts, only interpretations.

Nietzsche

2. How does philosophy work?

What is it?

Before presenting our philosophical model, we would like to show how philosophy works. We must first grasp not only the meaning and the value of philosophy but also the practical side of what we'll call the day-to-day philosophical work. Without that understanding, our model has no chance of achieving its objective, i.e. to help you live a better life.

We claim that no human being can live a day (an hour?) without making a reference, one way or another, to some kind of philosophical question. We are all philosophers, all the time; it's part of human nature.

Isn't it true that we wake up in the morning and start right away by asking ourselves some simple (and sometimes not so simple) questions, and already have some views on what's ahead of us, such as:

- What was the meaning of that weird dream I had last night?
- I wonder what's going to happen to me today?
- Why do I have to go and work?
- I really hate those mornings...
- How could I improve?
- I did not like that meeting yesterday with...?
- How can I get so-and-so to behave differently?
- I think I am going to fail again!
- Who can help me with this?
- I wish the day was already over...
- I wonder if what I did was wrong
- Et cetera...

Does this ring a bell? All those questions and comments do lead to some sort of philosophical thinking, as we'll see later.

So, we want to demystify philosophy and demonstrate that not only is it an easy (user-friendly) instrument, but that you are already using it, perhaps without knowing it.

What's in it for me?

It is very simple: a better understanding and hopefully a better control (use) of that very powerful tool which we call 'applied philosophy'. By the end of this chapter, you will:

1. Have a better comprehension of what you already do as a philosopher.
2. Identify some practical ways to improve your philosophical effectiveness.
3. Come up with some ideas on what else you could do to lead a better life.

What is the red thread?

Let's proceed step by step and see what we can get out of this chapter (please keep in mind that this is an introduction to the philosophical model we want to present afterwards):

This chapter will include the following questions and issues:

1. What does anybody's philosophical day look like?
2. What kind of a philosopher are you?
3. What are some of the 'deep' philosophical questions we should be concerned with?
4. What can we learn from the great philosophers?
5. How can I relate all of this to my life?

1. What does anybody's philosophical day look like?

Like yours, like mine! Nothing special, really. Let's briefly review our daily concerns and see how they can be philosophically analysed and understood:

MY PRIVATE LIFE

Let's pick up three typical worries that most people have and identify their philosophical dimensions:

Myself

- What am I going to do today?

This is related to the key question of the purpose of our day-to-day life. What should I do to make my day more worthwhile? Actions in a vacuum are purposeless and depressing. Behaviours within a framework are meaningful and more rewarding. So the philosophical question is, 'How can I make this day more *meaningful* for me?'

- Why am I not happier?

What a basic question! Many people have the feeling that they are not getting as much out of their lives as they should. They go through the motions of living, but it always seems that something is missing. In some cases they feel lonely and not quite satisfied with the quality of their lives. In others, they feel miserable and alienated. So they wake up in the morning and start the day with some heavy feelings and negative expectations. They know (intuitively) that there must be something else. They are lost. The philosophical aspect of this self-probing is:

What is the *value* of my daily life, and how can I make sure that what I do today will enhance my happiness?

- What's wrong with me?

This is a question that we all ask ourselves (one way or another) during the day. We question our abilities and sometimes our own identity. We are not satisfied with what (who) we are. We struggle with our behaviour and are sometimes amazed by what we do, the way we do it and the impact of our behaviour on ourselves as well as on others. We are at a loss. The image that we have of ourselves does not match our actions. This is again a fundamental philosophical issue: How come I am not what I would like to be? What's driving me? Who is in charge? It also leads to the question of freedom and responsibility!

Others

- How can they think and behave in that way?

This is about not being able to understand others. It is true (isn't it?) that there are times when we are puzzled and even shocked by other people's behaviour. We sometimes witness actions by others that are beyond our grasp. This (daily) observation has also a deep philosophical dimension, i.e. *what's right and what's wrong*? And, who decides on the acceptable and unacceptable ways of thinking and behaving?

- Why doesn't he/she love me?

Maybe the most frequently asked question of all! I love him (her) and there is nothing in return... Why? What can I do to get the other person's attention? Love? This is about relating to others and needing each other to live our lives. We cannot survive and be happy alone. We need to interact with others. We must give to and take from each other. We cannot just say to somebody we care about, 'Love me!' From a philosophical viewpoint, the issue is to understand why we need other people, and vice versa.

- Why are some people so selfish?

Many men and women suffer from others' behaviour. They perceive them as being unemotional, cold, distant and aggressive. You name it! Why? How is it that some people appear to be totally self-centred? It seems that some people have no reluctance whatsoever to use and manipulate others. They push and destroy. They just go ahead with their lives, not paying any attention (except if it is in their interest) to other people. The key philosophical questions here are: Why are some people so selfish? Am I selfish too? Is it wrong to be selfish? If so, why and to what extent?

MY PROFESSIONAL LIFE

Let's briefly examine three major life issues that we all face at work:

My job

Why is it that my job is not fulfilling any more? Once I loved it, but not any more. Why? This is a typical question that many people are asking today. What was exciting yesterday is boring today. There was a time when they went to the office quite early in the morning... and now they have to drag themselves to the place. Why? They feel that they are wasting their time, their lives. They say that they are not getting a fair chance to use their professional talents. And so it goes on. The key philosophical points here are: What is the meaning of work? Why should we spend so much time doing things that are not interesting and rewarding? Must we do it? In the name of what?

My career

Most men and women at work are also concerned about their professional ambitions and goals. They want a career. They want to succeed. And yet the fight and the competition are very intense. Many are interested and very few are successful. For many people that creates disappointment and frustration. So much energy and effort has been invested in the struggle for success that our patience shrinks and bad feelings step in. Is this a philosophical issue? Absolutely! Because it is connected with what we want to achieve with our life, the value of our efforts and the ultimate question, namely, 'What is this all about?'

The balance between my professional and private lives

So here you are in the middle of your life and now you're asking yourself: Was it worth it? Where is my family now? Where are the children? Did I see them grow? Was I around when they needed help? What have I done with my life? Were my values in order? What is success after all? Did I spend my time, energy and talents the 'right' way? These are basic philosophical interrogations that we should not address when it is too late!

Question

Please write down three of your own daily (or current) concerns and identify the philosophical dimension of each of them.

- My concern 1:
- My concern 2:
- My concern 3:

2. What kind of a philosopher are you?

So it seems that we are all philosophers confronted with the above questions (and many more, of course). This does not mean that we are all effective and bright philosophers. It depends on how good we are at:

1.   Asking the 'right' questions and probing the essence of our being.

     This requires courage. It means looking at our own relative and highly subjective ways of defining reality. It can be difficult to realise and accept that nothing exists for certain. It can be scary to face the fact that there is perhaps nothing but us with our dreams. It can be disturbing to see that yesterday's truth is today's lie!

2.   Spotting the right issues in relation to our existence.

     We cannot tackle all the questions of the world. We must be selective and single out what is vital for our survival as individuals. That must be done with a minimum of 'wisdom' if we want to progress and live a more meaningful life.

3.   Clarifying what they mean for us and other human (living?) beings.

     Nothing has meaning, in absolute terms, as we'll see later. Everything must be related to each individual. Philosophy is the art of deciding on the meanings of things, concepts and people. It is quite fascinating to see that we have the ability to look at the same things (inside and outside the human body) and come up with various interpretations of what it is.

4.   Exploring alternatives and deciding on what's best for us.

     The human mind is naturally curious. We constantly look for options. We probe and weigh our different ways of being. No human being is ever fully satisfied. Each of us has a fundamental need to move on and seek new paths of living. Many people like to see themselves as creative beings.

5.   Acting and getting results.

What's also fascinating is our individual ability to execute and transform some of our ideas and concepts into deeds, and by so doing impact on what is. At least, that's what we like to believe.

The four types of philosophers

There are, in our view, four main different types of philosophers. Of course, this is not necessarily the traditional classification that you will find in the textbooks, but we consider it to be a useful way of distinguishing the main currents of philosophical thought. Go through the exercise below and determine what is your personal approach to life (what kind of a philosopher are you?).

Please assess yourself going through each item and using the following scale: 1 for 'I never do this. It is not me' – 5 for 'Yes, I think and behave that way from time to time' – 10 for 'This is absolutely typical of me'. Feel free to pick up any number between 1 and 10 (e.g. 3.5 or 4.7 or 7). Add up your number for each set of items, and then look at the debriefing which follows.

PHILOSOPHER TYPE 1

I am the kind of person who likes to:

1. Learn by doing
2. Experience things by myself
3. Check and cross-check my understanding of things and people
4. Believe that facts exist
5. Experiment and try out things
6. Trust my senses and impressions
7. Observe and watch
8. Be pragmatic and down-to-earth
9. Implement and reflect on the results of my actions
10. Believe that reality exists independently from our minds, and also that we'll probably never get to know it as it is.

Add up all your scores and see now if you fit into this category.

For a score between 70 and 100, there is a good chance that you are what people sometimes categorise as *empirical* or *pragmatic*.

This kind of philosophy is characterised by the following:

- Your own life experience is what counts at the end of the day.

- Reality is to a large extent a result of our impressions of the world.

- The only thing we can do to know is to trust our senses and build our knowledge and behaviour on those impressions and how they affect us.

If you want to know more about this kind of philosophy, read the following philosophers, keeping in mind that sometimes only parts of their philosophical scheme belongs to this school of thought: Hume, Locke, Mill, Pierce, James and Dewey.

PHILOSOPHER TYPE 2

I am the kind of person who likes to:

1. Think before acting
2. Use my analytical skills in order to decide
3. Reason before reaching a conclusion
4. Understand why things are what they are
5. Be logical
6. Value systematic thinking and analysing
7. Believe that everything can be explained (or will be explained one day or another)
8. Trust the human ability to understand and even to give form to the world and its laws
9. Support the scientific way to approach reality
10. Think that the cause and effect law is critical to our understanding of the world.

Now add up all your scores and see if you belong to this category of philosophers.

For a score of between 70 and 100, you could be a *rational-*

ist or an *analytical* philosopher; that is, the kind of person who believes in the power of the rational, analytical mind.

Rationalists believe in:

- The power of the human brain (reason) to create forms, patterns that will give meaning to our perceptions of the world. For such thinkers, for instance, the so-called natural laws of the universe are nothing else than our own human way of understanding what goes on before us, and do not at all necessarily reflect an objective reality that exists independently of us.

- Most rationalists think that the part of our knowledge that thus gives meaning to our perceptions is innate, and common to all human beings.

Some rationalists, pushing the argument further, go as far as saying that the only reality is what we produce in our minds. These philosophers are referred to as idealists. For the extreme idealist, 'the real is the rational'.

For more on this type of philosophy, consult mainly but not exclusively: Descartes, Spinoza, Berkeley, Kant, Leibniz and Hegel.

PHILOSOPHER TYPE 3

I am the kind of person who likes to:

1. Question everything, including well-established rules of conduct
2. Look for ways to promote justice and fairness
3. Work out how we can have a better life in this world
4. Spend time on deciding what's right and what's wrong
5. Make sure that my actions are in line with a set of ethical values
6. Be true to myself
7. Reflect on the best way to conduct my life
8. Recognise my flaws
9. Probe the issue of freedom
10. Invest time and energy in the pursuit of happiness.

For a score of between 70 and 100, you may be a *moralist* or a strong adherent of Socrates and his followers. You are very much concerned about the rights and wrongs of human life. You are always seeking for a better way to act and serve humanity.

Moralists are philosophers who:

- Care about basic moral issues such as justice, truth, fairness, dignity and freedom.

- Look for better answers to the challenge of living on earth.

- Are generally more concerned about our way of *living* than about our way of *knowing* (although of course, one does not go without the other...).

To go deeper into this way of practising philosophy, read: Epicurus, Plato, Kant (again, but he has more than one facet!), Nietzsche, Kierkegaard and Schopenhauer.

PHILOSOPHER TYPE 4

I am the kind of person who likes to:

1. Think that philosophy exists to serve humankind
2. Believe in my social responsibility
3. Trust our ability to work together to explain what the world is all about
4. Value human relations and solidarity very much
5. Question the distribution of power in human societies
6. Look for social justice and fairness
7. Fight for new and better ways to live together
8. Invest time and energy in improving our concepts of social and economic development
9. Challenge ethical codes created by the 'elite' for the sake of their self-interest
10. Assume that we are all equals.

If your score is between 70 and 100, you are definitely what can be called a *social* or *political* philosopher. Social or political philosophers are not at all concerned with the understanding of the world for its own sake. They want to know more, in order to improve the quality of our social or community life. They think and fight for:

- A better balance of power between the key social players.
- More social justice and equality.
- Involving people in their definition of reality, as it leads to a specific form of social organisation.

The main philosophers who developed and used this approach are the Stoics, Plato, Voltaire, Rousseau, Diderot and Marx.

Question

Assuming that you have scored quite highly in more than one category, what does it make you? Think about it.

3. What are some of the 'deep' philosophical questions I should be concerned with?

It seems that philosophers have always been struggling with three major questions:

Question 1. What is it, or what is the meaning of something (whatever)?

This question is really the bottom-line issue. We cannot live in a senseless world. We must identify things and give them an identity (or acknowledge what they are in themselves), so that we can understand and use them. As we said before, nothing exists for us human beings *per se*. Everything must have a label and a meaning. Actually, we could even go as far as saying that as long as something does not have a name, it does not exist for us! (See Wittgenstein and his use of linguistics as a philosophical instrument.) Think about:

- Cancer
- Atoms
- The subconscious

This leads us to three extremely important sub-questions for our daily life:

- Is the name the thing?
- What happens if I change the name of the thing?
- Do we change the very nature of something by naming it in a certain way?

Question 2. How do I know that something is what I think it is?

This is a powerful question. This is obviously related to the process by which we create our knowledge as we discussed it in Chapter 1. Could it be that the proper answer is that we can never know for sure? The various types of philosophers that we mentioned have over time come up with their best answers, and they differ:

- The **pragmatists** say that we know because it is working, and experience has shown us that we can rely on it. It is a question of relying on our own impressions as well as what our experience of life has taught us.

- The **rationalists** claim that we know when our mind (our reasoning) can prove that our way of thinking and behaving is consistent, and that we can predict what will be the result of any given event or action.

- The **moralists** are primarily concerned about how we conduct our lives and whether they should conform to transcendent rules that we must abide by or to conditions for happiness that we have determined through our best intellectual efforts. Moralists will continuously challenge the given codes of ethics in a constant effort to discover and justify the best possible ways of behaving.

- The **social/political** philosophers believe that what counts most is the balance of power in our societies. These thinkers will try to identify the forces (economic, political, moral, religious) that give form to societies, and will seek for ways to improve social structures and organisations so as to ensure the maximum welfare and happiness to the people involved.

Question 3. Why is it what it is and not something else?

This is the difficult question. Why are things (including us) what they are and not something else? What else could there be anyway? Why do we exist? Why am I here? Why do we see the world the way we see it? Why am I the person that I am? Why do I behave the way I do? Why business? Why power? Why... and we could go on and on with the 'why' question.

Nobody has an absolute answer. There are four basic approaches to answer any fundamental 'why' questions (revisiting our section on knowledge):

- The **scientific** way: Involves looking for the physical causes of what is and understanding the relationship between cause and effect. Stop questioning when the cause gets out of reach (experimentation). This is the objective way, and it accepts all the answers whatever they are (as long as they fit...).

- The **religious** way: God is the origin of everything, and faith in the divine message will give the answer to any 'why' question.

- The **philosophical** way: The process of asking the questions and of coming up with some rational answers. The process itself is telling us something important about ourselves. The answers are part of what we are.

- Finally, the fourth way, which is the '**common sense**' one used by most people in their lives, and that is to take those big questions one at a time, see how we can answer with our own limited means, or just accept the answers that were passed on to us by family, education or tradition, and move on with what we can afford. The problem with this approach is that it leaves room for a lot of haziness, loose ends and unanswered parts, which not everybody can easily live with for very long.

Question (for you, the reader)

What is the question that we have not mentioned? Think hard... harder!

4. What can we learn from the great philosophers?

It is not the purpose of this book to review the considerable contributions of the great philosophers over the centuries.

However, we would like to point out some of the concerns shared by quite a few of the greatest minds of our human history:

1. THE ISSUE OF TRUTH

Most philosophers have tackled the truth question at a certain point in their lives. It seems that we cannot escape from this question: What is the truth? Does it exist? If it does, how do we access it?

The answers vary from 'God is the truth' (a transcendent answer, which is not quite a philosophical one since it relies on an act of faith) to 'The truth is what a human mind can discover through its analytical capabilities'. Some philosophers also believe that every human being, with his or her answers to life, however he or she reached them, holds the truth.

Questions for you:

1. What is your own definition of the truth?
2. How much do you value it?
3. How does it impact your daily life?

2. THE ISSUE OF FREEDOM

This is also a recurrent question asked by the philosophers of all times: Are we free? What does it mean to be free? Can we really decide on what course of action we should take? Do we have a choice? Can we be different from what we are? Can we really change what we are deep down inside?

Philosophers throughout the centuries have approached the freedom issue from three different angles:

- **Approach 1**: The freedom to be what we want to be, to decide on what the world is about and model it according to our wishes or will. We call this *total freedom*. Needless to say, we need to think deeply to realise that there are a lot of things which exist in the world and are beyond our control.

- **Approach 2**: The freedom to decide among a set of predetermined options. In other words, we have choices. We are not free to decide on what we are and are becoming. It seems however that we have various alternatives and options for achieving what's imposed on us. We call this *partial freedom*.

- **Approach 3**: There is no freedom whatsoever. Freedom is an illusion or wishful thinking. We, as human beings, are predetermined by our biological make-up as well as by education and other circumstances. The only thing we can do is to accept and enjoy (if and when possible...) what we are. We call this *predetermination*.

Questions for you:

1. Do you perceive yourself as a free human being?
2. What do you really do with your freedom? How do you use it?
3. Can you identify three things that you cannot exercise freedom in? What is this telling you about the very nature and value of freedom?

3. THE ISSUE OF BEAUTY

It is extraordinary that we all have the capability of determining whether something (somebody) is beautiful or not. The question is then: What is the meaning of aesthetics? What do we mean by 'This is beautiful'? So many thoughts, feelings and behaviours are determined by that sense of grace and beauty. This leads us to the question of art and the artistic dimension of our life.

Many philosophers have devoted time and energy in the exploration of aesthetics and art. It is interesting to briefly see how philosophy probed this question:

- Some philosophers viewed art as an escape from the harshness of reality. It is basically a way of reaching a state of peace and contentment that cannot be found in 'real' life.

- Others looked at art as being an important contribution of the human psyche in the construction of reality. By inventing beauty, we bring something to reality that was not there before. There is an added value. An artistic creation is closer to what *is* than our analytical thoughts or our direct perceptions of the world.

Questions for you:

1. How important is art for you?

2. Can you identify the impact of beauty on your life (in general)?

3. Do you pay any attention to music, painting, literature, poetry or other forms of artistic work? Why? What do you get out of it?

5. HOW CAN I RELATE ALL OF THIS TO MY LIFE?

Philosophy applies to everything we think, feel and do. How can we live without asking some questions about what's happening inside and outside our bodies?

A philosophical approach to life is just common sense. We cannot stop ourselves from pondering on what we are and do, but also – and more importantly – on why we are what we are.

The question is really: How can philosophy help us live a better life and become better leaders of others (the main theme of this book)?

Let's answer that question by asking you, the reader, to check on the following proposals (please put a tick next to the items that you agree with).

Do you think that it would be good and valuable to have a friendly instrument that would help you:

1. Ask the important questions

   So often we waste time and energy asking irrelevant questions or questions which are not that important for us. We struggle with unimportant or irrelevant issues and get lost in the resolution of false problems. We wander and get swamped in trivial arguments.

   – Tick here if you agree:

   Well, it seems that philosophy provides the framework that we need to make sure that we really concentrate on (ask) the 'right' questions, i.e. the ones that make sense for us and are critical for the management of our lives.

2. Put things into perspective

    We need to look at our life events with a sense of relativity. It is so easy for us human beings to get deeply involved in crises and dramatic moments that actually are not very important. We get overwhelmed and lose our sense of sound judgement. We lack the ability to put things, people and events into context.

    –   Tick here if you agree:

    Philosophy certainly provides a framework that we can use to put things into context and evaluate our daily experiences.

3. Decide on priorities and focus

    How many times have we gotten involved in activities that after all were not very high on our life list? Isn't it true that we have missed good life opportunities because we were doing something already (not so important)? The point is that we all have a tendency to be unfocused or to lose sight of things that are important for us. We lack concentration and consistency in the investment of our time and talents.

    –   Tick here if you agree:

    We need some guidelines that we can use to decide on our priorities and actions. We must make sure that we do things that are truly vital for us. That is also something that philosophy offers.

4. Understand what is happening to me

    Isn't it true that very often we do not understand what is going on in our life? We are at a loss with ourselves. We do not have the proper tools for understanding why we are who we are. Our own behaviours and actions surprise us. Our own emotions and feelings puzzle us. We are strangers to ourselves. (And all of this applies of course to our perception of and interaction with others.)

    –   Tick here if you agree:

    As we shall see later in the book, this is exactly what philosophy can give us: a systematic way to identify, analyse and understand our emotions and behaviours.

5. Behave to maximise my happiness

   Here is the ultimate question: How can I make myself happy? What must I do to make my life more meaningful and myself happier? The question is not so much about being different as exploiting what we have and using it in such a way that we feel good about our life.

   – Tick here if you agree:

   Philosophy is about wisdom – or the art of being happy, whatever the circumstances are. Philosophy aims at giving each of us what is required to live a meaningful and very happy life. It starts with who we are and what we have. In many cases, it stops there.

6. Live with a sense of order

   So often we have a feeling that we are being pushed around at random, that nothing makes sense. We lack a good reference that will allow us to live with a minimum of coherence and stability. We are lost and lack the required support to make sense of our own life.

   – Tick here if you agree:

   Philosophy provides a way to decide on that very much needed reference. It helps us reflect and decide on it for the sake of our own balance.

Well, count now how many times you said, 'Yes, I agree.' If it is more than four times, we believe you should proceed with your reading. Between two and four, it could benefit you to go back a little bit and review what we have covered so far before proceeding. Under two means it is perhaps time to ask yourself if you really want to go ahead with this book!

What are the leadership implications?

It seems highly important for a leader to understand the philosophical dimensions of human life. That comprehension includes:

1. Acknowledging what kind of a leadership philosopher he or she is

2. Paying attention to the philosophical side of his or her team members or colleagues at work

3. Investing time and energy in the handling of the three critical issues, i.e. truth, freedom and beauty (and ethics, of course, but that will be part of a special chapter).

YOU AS A LEADER AND A PHILOSOPHER

There is no question that your philosophical profile has a strong impact on the way you tackle challenges and manage people:

The pragmatic leader-philosopher: Down-to-earth, you address challenges in a straightforward way and manage people equally, i.e. in a factual, no-nonsense style. Knowing is good enough for you. Facts speak for themselves and should be enough to convince people to do what they are supposed to do.

The rationalist leader-philosopher: You like to understand why things and people are what they are. You then build strategies and plans to move forward and get the people with you. You need to get to the causes of things before deciding anything.

The moralist leader-philosopher: What is right and wrong is an issue you have in mind. You want to be fair to people. You are concerned with the creation (and use) of the proper code of conduct so that people feel that your expectations are legitimate.

The social/political leader-philosopher: 'Power' and 'network' are two key words for you. You aim at making sure that the social environment is conducive to good deeds and results. You believe in the need for power to accomplish great outcomes.

YOU AS A LEADER AND A CREATIVE LISTENER

Creative leaders are quite good at 'reading' people. They are particularly efficient at doing three things:

1. Understanding how different people think. They are proficient at deciphering other people's thought processes without falling into the '*attribution trap*' which is to explain other individuals' behaviours by using one's own frame of reference. (This is called 'empathy' by the OB people.)

2. Reaching out and transforming a simple exchange of information into a creative act. They take advantage of

the words – and the ideas – used or presented by the other party to add some values to the exchange and make it special and unique. We call this '*creative listening*'.

3. Communicating more effectively by *formatting their messages* so that they match the main reference of the individual they are talking to.

YOU AS A CREATOR OF MEANINGS

Most people do care about the three following philosophical issues, i.e. truth, freedom and beauty.

- **Truth:** There are so many lies in so many organisations. Leaders must learn how to be much more straightforward with the people. What's at stake here is their leadership credibility.

- **Freedom:** Research shows that many people in many teams and companies want more space for initiatives. They want more freedom for thinking and acting. They want to be trusted. They want to be judged on the basis of the results they get – not on their intentions or even their input. They want to be left alone (at least from time to time).

- **Beauty:** Yes, beauty is also becoming a high value asset in the working place. A lot of men and women want to work in clean and nice environments. They care about the physical place where they work. They appreciate a leader who is able to invest time, energy and money in the architecture and design of their offices. It seems that there is a growing expectation among the new generation regarding the beauty of forms and space. Arts are getting into the workplace!

One conclusion we can draw from the above points is that the leaders of tomorrow are going to have to be creative by:

- re-inventing themselves (not only having flexibility in their styles but also invention in their mindsets);

- being creative listeners ('Let's invent each other'); and

- investing more time and energy in the aesthetic part of their roles (art and work).

3. The Project-to-Live: I am my reference

What is it?

This part of the book is about the need for a reference (we called it a 'yardstick' in Chapter 1) in order to decide on the meaning of anything. No reference, no meaning. In other words, people, events and things mean something according to the reference we use. It is essential then to realise what the ultimate reference is for us human beings. It is absolutely critical for all of us to know what our ultimate personal reference is. It determines the sense of our lives and the main orientations of our actions. This is what this chapter is all about. By the same token, we will introduce, via the reference concept, our *philosophical model*.

What's in it for me?

Nobody can live without a reference – including you, the reader. So, what is your ultimate reference? Do you know it? Is it one that you chose? Or was it (is it) imposed on you? Is it a good one? Is it the best for you? How does your reference affect your life? Again, is it something that you want? Do you have a choice? What are your options?

These are some of the questions that this chapter will explore. We are really talking here about the foundations of your life. Isn't it worth a chapter or one hour of your time? We claim that we can only see what our reference allows us to see. So, understanding and managing our reference is vital in order to have a 'good' life.

What is the red thread?

The chapter will cover the following questions and issues:

1. What is a reference?

2. How does a reference work?
3. Has the reference evolved over time?
4. What reference is appropriate for today?
5. The Project-to-Live as the ultimate reference of meaning.

1. What is a reference?

A reference is what's behind everything we think and do. It explains what we experience and how important it is. A simple illustration will clarify this concept.

What is money? The answer could be:

- A means to succeed in life
- A reward for a job well done
- A necessary evil
- A survival tool
- A must to be appreciated by others
- Power
- Et cetera.

Behind each concept, we can find a different reference, namely success, career, God, survival, status, ambitions. The same word will mean quite a few different things according to the references we use.

Think about it: a reference is basically what enables me to determine the meaning of something. With or without our being aware of it, we refer what we see, experience, love, enjoy and hate to a series of intermediary references that we finally relate to a fundamental or ultimate reference.

Philosophy is geared at identifying and eventually deciding on that last resort reference that we want to use to make sense of our life.

We must realise that all our thoughts, feelings and behaviours are indeed connected to some intermediary references which are in turn dependent on the basic reference.

Our life makes sense because there is a reference behind everything we do.

Let's summarise:

1. No meaning without a reference;

2. Our daily activities are always related to some intermediary references; and

3. There is always an ultimate reference behind all the intermediary references.

2. How does a reference work?

When we look at something (someone), we immediately come up with an explanation of what it is (or who he/she is). We always identify what we see. We label it. We define it.

Sometimes it is not so simple or so obvious and we have to work on it.

The point however is that we always define what we perceive according to a set of basic yardsticks which can all be related to an ultimate foundation that we call 'the reference'.

When we say 'this is that' or 'this means that' we always make a reference to something else that we already know. There is no meaning from scratch. Things do not exist in a vacuum. 'This' will have a meaning only in relation to another thing that I have previously encountered (or speculated about) and integrated into my idea of the world.

There can be no meaning without a reference to which what we see can be anchored. One must realise that the prior establishment of a reference on which it can be founded (as we talked about before) conditions knowledge.

No reference, no knowledge!

Question

Do you accept the idea: No knowledge without a reference?

The reference that we adopt or create determines our entire understanding of the world and of our existence. We are our reference or, more precisely, we are what our chosen reference determines us to think, believe and do.

It is then important to (keep your pencil handy, please):

1. Be aware of the reference I use in my life (not just the intermediary references but rather the ultimate refer-

ence). I see what my reference allows me to see. I value things and people according to my reference. I organise my life according to it.

- – 'I HAVE MY PERSONAL REFERENCE'

2. Understand the reference that other people use as well as the potential conflicts (and opportunities) that the differences in the reference can lead to.

- – 'THEY HAVE THEIR OWN REFERENCES'

3. Learn how to manage our reference (and intermediary references) so that we maximise the quality of our understanding of the world and ourselves. The reference is open to questioning and alteration. We must decide on what we want to use so that what we see makes sense to us. (A basic philosophical issue: Can human beings freely decide on their reference?)

- – 'WE ARE RESPONSIBLE FOR OUR REFERENCE'

4. Invent processes by which we discuss our different references without going to war and destroying each other. We must not only accept that we see things differently but also that our foundations for meaning are sometimes very far apart. Actually, we need to be different so that we can be more creative. Can you imagine a world with people having precisely the same perceptions, views and values?

- – 'WE MUST BE TOLERANT'

5. Realise that the fundamental search for the ultimate reference is the most meaningful quest for us human beings. We must keep working on the probing of our fundamental reference because that is what determines our humanity.

- – 'WE MUST KEEP SEARCHING'

Here are our key points:

We interpret the internal and external worlds according to our ultimate reference. There is no meaning without a reference. We naturally use a lot of intermediary references in our day-to-day lives. However, those sub-anchor points are all related one way or another to the final reference that we call the foundation of meaning. That last resort reference is what counts because it determines all the other reference points.

Let's have a look at another simple illustration: Why do I work so hard? The analysis of that question can lead to the identification of some intermediary references and then to the foundation of meaning, which in this case could look like this:

Intermediary references

I work because:

- I need the money (money)
- My family needs it (family)
- I enjoy my work (personal satisfaction)
- I'll succeed through my hard work (success)
- I'll be promoted (power).

Ultimate references

I work because:

- It's a condition for my survival (I am the reference)
- God expects me to work hard (God is the reference)
- It is required by the collective (The social body is the reference).

A pause is in order here. Does the concept of the reference (ultimate and intermediary) make sense to you (so far)?

We think that it would be good for you, the reader, to put down the book for a few minutes and just react to the following sentences:

- My perception of the ultimate reference today is quite different from what it was when I was young.
- My spouse's intermediary references (reference?) are quite different from mine.
- Many conflicts, confrontations and wars can be explained because of the differences in references.

3. Has the reference evolved over time?

A more effective way to understand the concept of the reference is to look at how it has evolved over time. Here is a brief history of the 'metaphysical reference of meaning'. (You can skip this part if you are not at all interested in the history of philosophy.)

A BRIEF HISTORY OF THE REFERENCE (LEARNING FROM SOME OF THE PHILOSOPHICAL GIANTS)

The history of the quest for the ultimate reference can to a large extent be assimilated to the history of Western thought, going from the Presocratic philosophers to how we think predominantly today. During that period, the reference has accomplished an extraordinary voyage, which took it away from – and finally back to – *man*, thus completing a gigantic cycle that lasted more than twenty centuries.

Protagoras

We shall start the story of this voyage with Protagoras, a thinker who lived in the fifth century BC. Protagoras, of whose writings there remains very little, has nevertheless left us with this lapidary sentence of utmost importance: 'Man is the measure of all things.'

By that, what Protagoras was telling us was that man, as a thinking being, was naturally led to establish himself as the ultimate foundation of the meaning that he conferred to all things, and hence to the world as such and to his own existence.

What Protagoras, however, did not define, was what he meant exactly by 'man'. Indeed, what is this *man* that confers a meaning to all things? A body? A mind? A soul? By leaving the notion of 'man' undetermined in its essence, Protagoras opened the way to a vast amount of philosophical thinking that was to take place in the centuries that followed him.

Plato

Plato, coming shortly after Protagoras, denied that man could be of his own self the measure of all things, and undertook to drive the reference of meaning not only far from man himself, but also away from man's world.

The reference henceforth took for Plato the form of an *idea* or *form* that represented the 'real' world, of which our world here below was to be seen as nothing more than a pale and degraded image.

Man was no more entitled to pass a judgement on things in relation to his self. Plato invited him instead to discover the meaning of the phenomena of this 'virtual' world by relating them to the ideas (forms) of the 'real' world, of which, according to Plato, he fortunately kept within himself some form of memory or innate knowledge.

Thus did Plato split the world in two and in such a forceful and persuasive way that this duality of the worlds continues to deeply impregnate our culture even today.

This Platonic dualistic vision was logically adopted and perpetuated by the *Christian religion* (as well as by the other monotheistic religions), for which a God, creator of the world and of man and therefore located outside of these creations, replaced the idea as the foundation of meaning. For the Christian man, truth was in God and in His revealed speech, and by extension in the doctrine extrapolated from this speech by the Fathers of the Church. If he wished to understand the meaning of things, the man of faith was encouraged to interpret them in relation to the sacred texts.

Descartes

Descartes was the thinker who, in the seventeenth century, opened the most significant breach in this dual construction of the worlds that had been established by Plato and prolonged by the Churches.

Descartes undertook to hand back to man the privilege of deciding on his own on the meaning of things. With Descartes, man's reason became the foundation of meaning, the ultimate reference.

However, Descartes did not fully distance himself from the Christian way of thinking, for whilst the Cartesian man was entitled and even encouraged to think for himself, his judgement remained subject to divine validation, as God continued to be viewed as the guarantor of the 'clear and distinct' quality of man's ideas.

Still, with Descartes the reference had re-entered the world and man, and the thinkers that succeeded him were to pursue this inexorable return to the original way of thinking of Protagoras.

Kant

Kant, for his part, by extending much further the role that Descartes had attributed to man's reason in defining the meaning of things, ended up establishing the ultimate reference of meaning completely within the human mind.

This is not to say that Kant denied the possibility of transcendence. Indeed, he even adopted Plato's view that our world was but a world of phenomena, and that the 'real world' was other. But Kant also explained that anything that stood beyond our natural world of experience, be it the 'real world' or even God, was not accessible to our knowledge, since we could not grasp it through our natural senses (no possible perception). Therefore any metaphysical concept that we chose to use as an ultimate reference for understanding the world was to be considered as a pure view of the mind, a sheer 'idea' of our reason. *Since the existence of God Himself could not be experienced, it could only be the subject of our belief or faith.*

With Kant, we thus end up with the reference of meaning having reintegrated not only the world but man himself, in whose reason it is now entirely embedded. There remains however an unbridgeable gap between man's understanding of the natural world and his idealistic view of the ultimate foundation of meaning, which is a matter of speculation or faith.

It was the task of Kant's followers to reunite the world of ideas and the world of phenomena into one single natural world, as well as to modify the location within man of the ultimate foundation of meaning. It would indeed become more and more evident with time that it is not within our reason that lies our most essential essence, but somewhere deeper in our physical being. That is precisely what Schopenhauer undertook to accomplish, and after him Nietzsche.

Schopenhauer and Nietzsche

Schopenhauer, to begin with, rejected Kant's notion of the duality of the worlds, and asserted that indeed the world was only one and that its form could be identified as that of a *will*.

Thus the world as a whole and every one of its parts were but different figures of one sole and same will, which could be pictured as a sort of force directed towards nothing else than its own expansion. For things to be understood, they needed to be related to this notion of will, which stood thereon as the ultimate foundation of meaning.

As for Nietzsche, he adopted this notion of will and transformed it into what he called the '*will for power*'.

Since man himself was now a ramification of the will or the 'will for power', one might at first sight deduce that he was hence reinstalled as the reference of meaning, and that we had eventually rejoined Protagoras. That was not yet the case, however, for in Schopenhauer's and Nietzsche's views the will continues to transcend man and to encompass the world in its entirety, of which man is but a part. To understand things, therefore, man is still obliged to refer to a notion which exceeds him and of which he is not the unique holder.

One can nevertheless observe that with Schopenhauer, as well as with Nietzsche, the essence of man (which is the same as the essence of the world) has become 'will' instead of 'reason'. This evolution is absolutely crucial, for it opens the way for a positioning of the foundation of meaning in a place within man which may be considered as more essential than the mere seat of his thought.

With Schopenhauer and Nietzsche, the reference of meaning is now *within* the world (the will), both *external and internal* (a will in general and man's volition in particular) and *single* (one supreme will). It still transcends man, however, since man is only a ramification of the will in general, which is given as the essence of the world.

Before we can really consider as closed the great loop which will bring us back to Protagoras, i.e. to man, we shall still need to disassociate the ultimate reference of meaning from any notion that would still transcend man, such as ideas, God, the will or the will for power. We must do it in such a way that the meaning which we give to the world can be founded in the very essence of what constitutes us as living beings.

Nietzsche shocked the world by proclaiming that 'God is dead' (implying by this that the notion of a supernatural being had to a great extent lost its magic power to provide a credible meaning to the world).

Many people misunderstood him and were not able to accept that major shift in their reference. They still attempted to give to the ultimate reference of meaning a transcending status.

Let us mention here the great political ideologies of which

the finality was supposed to supersede that of the individual, and which eventually turned into the disasters that we know, or indeed other transcending notions such as progress, technology, pragmatism, money or even love as a universal value.

What we propose in this book is to restore man to his full dignity as a living, thinking being, which had been granted to him more that twenty centuries ago by Protagoras.

We believe that we must cease to refer, when understanding the world in which we live, to a foundation of meaning which supersedes it and by the same token supersedes us.

Although we can recognise the value of this transcendence from a historical perspective, we are also convinced that it can no more satisfy us with a rational all encompassing understanding of the world. That is why we shall submit in this book that the ultimate reference of a rational meaning of the world is man himself, and it is in his power alone to fully establish and demonstrate his understanding of all things, and hence of his own life.

Question

How do you react to this brief review of the history of the reference? Can you summarise the key phases of its evolution?

4. What reference is appropriate for today?

Our contention is that we have reached a point in history when it is time to give back to man what Protagoras, more than 2,000 years ago, had already endowed him with: 'Man is the measure of all things'!

We think that man possesses the full responsibility and ability to establish on his own and in relation to himself the meaning of the world as such and of his own life.

This implies that the ultimate philosophical reference lies within man himself and no more in any way beyond him or her. As we have seen above, this is only a validation of the historical movement that has taken us from the Platonic Ideas to God, then back to our reason and finally to our will.

We propose to call this ultimate foundation of meaning the 'Project-to-Live', signifying by that that the essence of man as a living being is in fact his *life* itself, viewed as a purpose, as a will – in other words as the original intention of all our intentions.

The next section will describe the Project-to-Live and show how it can help us understand all the things that comprise the world, including ourselves, what we feel and what we do.

5. The Project-to-Live as the ultimate reference of meaning

We have posed the ultimate foundation of meaning of the world as well as of our existence as being the Project-to-Live. The underlying purpose of this project can be expressed as follows:

'Life is a project – the project of its own perpetuation. To live is to want to live.'

Stop! Can you please challenge the idea that 'to live is to want to live'!

From this premise, we can deduce that the significance of any object, any event or any behaviour can be explained in terms of its final purpose, which is always the individual's will for self-perpetuation.

Or, to put it differently, things have a meaning for me only according to my PTL, which is fundamentally characterised by my need to preserve and expand my life. It is me and only me!

Basing ourselves on this proposition, we will endeavour to demonstrate that it is possible to understand all our doings through that ultimate reference. Our claim is that we do what we do in order to accomplish our Projects-to-Live, or ensure the perpetuation of our lives.

We are aware that such a claim can appear at first as being limited and constrictive. We shall attempt to prove that, on the contrary, our foundation gives us the possibility of encompassing all the various aspects of life, including what it has to offer, as being the most generous, noble and even sublime.

The key characteristics of the Project-to-Live can be identified as follows:

Our Project-to-Live is our very being; it is us, each one of us. Therefore we are entitled to say: '*I am my Project-to-Live and I understand the world and everything that it comprises (including my existence) inasmuch as they affect this project.*'

The challenge that we all face is to realise that we are only conscious of our own personal Project-to-Live. Nothing authorises us to assert *a priori* that other people, our fellow beings, are also driven by the same project as us, which is merely to live. This is even more challenging when you consider that all the individual Projects-to-Live manifest themselves in their own specific way. Each person conceives things and events in relation to how they affect his or her Project-to-Live. Each individual is, from his or her own perspective, 'the measure of all things', as Protagoras stated.

However, as we appear to each other identically alive and since we are able to communicate between ourselves, we are also able to confirm to one another that we do indeed share the same fundamental Project-to-Live. We all apparently have the same essence, which is the will to perpetuate our lives. It is this mutual assumption and recognition that we are all fellow beings engaged in the same project which leads us to understand and feel for the next person.

Because our first and foremost priority is our personal PTL, one has to accept that we must be and are indeed intrinsically selfish. My main concern is to perpetuate my own existence, and all the rest comes later and can only be taken into consideration in the ranking order according to which it impacts my personal PTL.

This fundamental principle may at first sight appear shocking, but only because it goes against the cultural background in which we have all been educated and which preaches generosity, love for one another and self-sacrifice. If we dare to listen to our deepest aspiration, there is no doubt that the most intimate message we will hear is:

'Care for your life. Keep on living.'

This does not mean, however, that we should be or are insensitive to others. In fact, it's quite the other way around.

We have an instinctive tendency to care for our fellow humans and are willing to give up a lot to help them in their own PTL. We must realise that the feeling we have for others stems from our being aware of the fact that all our fellow humans (as well as all other living beings, incidentally) share the same will to live as we do, which generates this feeling of solidarity between us all. We are indeed predominantly self-centred, but we are also conscious of the PTL of our brothers and sisters and feel for it. This universality of essence is what leads to our ethical conduct which, as we shall see later, does not in any way negate our selfishness but rather builds on it and even turns it into magnanimity when and as we feel it opportune.

Our Project-to-Live is a complex system that tends to perpetuate its own existence. It is made of three elements that can be labelled as:

- the *essence* of our PTL, which we call our Will-to-Live:
    - 'I AM WHAT DRIVES ME'
- the *means* by which our PTL is accomplished, which we call our Power-to-Live:
    - 'I AM WHAT I AM CAPABLE OF'
- the actual *implementation* of our Project-to-Live, which we call our Way-to-Live:
    - 'I AM WHAT I DO' and 'I AM WHAT I FEEL'

We shall be careful as we move on not to confuse the Project-to-Live as we have just defined it with the multiple projects of all sorts that we fulfil daily during our existence.

Our Project-to-Live has no other finality than its own perpetuation as such. Each one of our other various projects, on the other hand, tends towards an end, a final result to be achieved, the purpose of which will be of course to contribute for its part to the realisation of our overall Project-to-Live.

In other words, while we undertake all the projects of our existence with the intention of leading them to their term, as regards our Project-to-Live it is in no way its end but its mere perpetuation as such that we aim for. In fact, the only end that we can conceive for our Project-to-Live is our death, which is of course the very negation of the intent that underlies it.

From this we can observe again that are we all identical in the sense that we have in common the same Will-to-Live which characterises us in our essence as living beings. We are also all different by virtue of the multitude of the specific sub-projects that we carry out during our existence – due to the diversity of our respective Powers-to-Live and of our behaviours, in other words of our Way-to-Live – in order to ensure, each one of us as he may, the perpetuation of our individual PTL.

Question

Without looking at the text above, can you summarise your understanding of what the Project-to-Live is about. We challenge you to remember at least three ideas related to the PTL concept:

1.

2.

3.

Got them all... and more...? You do not have to agree (particularly at this initial stage)!

WHAT ARE THE LEADERSHIP IMPLICATIONS?

More on the notion of the reference, but this time with a historical perspective and the presentation of a philosophical model that we call the 'Project-to-Live' (PTL).

Leaders who want to improve their performance can use the introduction to the PTL idea and focus, for instance, on:

- The need for more leadership tolerance
- The challenge from great philosophers
- The impact of the PTL on leadership performance.

LEADERSHIP TOLERANCE

It is clear that different people have various views regarding common issues and questions. As we all know this is both good (it leads to creativity) and bad (it leads to conflicts). The responsibility of the leader is to:

- Make sure that the differences in individual references do not trigger destructive confrontations.

- Encourage the use of various references to look at the same situation so that it leads to better understanding of what it is all about.

- Manage the variety of references so that it produces new ideas.

- Avoid the excess of tolerance (a source of chaos and inaction).

LEADERSHIP IDEAS FROM GREAT PHILOSOPHERS

Here is a selection of ideas for leadership actions (even better, create your own list):

Protagoras: Consider each of your team members as an ultimate reference, i.e. someone who has a unique way of looking at the world and contributing to its enhancement.

Listen to each person as if he or she held the truth.

Plato: Remember that for Plato, this world in which we live is only a reflection of the real world of forms which lies out there somewhere in limbo.

So one could say that a Platonic leader would be one who has the vision of an ideal form of the business and works to transform present reality so as to bring it to match his vision.

A Platonic leader will tend to work from a pre-designed blueprint, rather than proceed through a trial and error reforming method.

Descartes: If you cannot measure it, then forget it.

Hume: The pragmatic, empirical leader will trust in his or her senses and rely on what 'works'. It's no use imagining ideal situations, they never exist in the 'real' world. This type of leader likes to deal with facts more than with ideas.

Schopenhauer: Recognise the power of the will. Identify the natural flow of the energy within the team (or organisation) and use it to support your own action. Go with the flow.

Nietzsche: Encourage each individual to take charge of himself or herself. Value personal autonomy, responsibility and freedom of action. Make each team member accountable to himself or herself.

PTL LEADERSHIP

If each individual is a Project-to-Live, then leaders must:

- Know what a PTL is,
- Be ready to identify with each team member, and
- Acknowledge what makes each person different.

Every thing that is tends to persevere in its being.

Baruch Spinoza

4. The Will-to-Live: I am what drives me

What is it?

There is something in everybody that determines the very nature of life as well as its value. It is something that all beings share in common. It is the basic drive that makes us what we are and (incidentally) perpetuates life on the planet. Some people would call it the essence of our being. We call it the **Will-to-Live**.

What's in it for me?

Take a few minutes to go through this chapter to really grasp what the human common denominator is. We are going to challenge you with some provocative ideas related to human nature. We'll claim that in a way (an important one!) we are all alike. We all have the same basic will: the Will-to-Live. We'll shortly introduce a new concept, i.e. the energy factor in your life, or what we call the 'Vitality Quotient'. You will reflect on the very nature, quality and intensity of your own drive. Maybe you will be surprised!

What is the red thread?

We'll look here at what drives us all. We shall do it step by step by reviewing the following questions and issues:

1. What is the Will-to-Live?
2. My Will-to-Live as the ultimate reference
3. The Will-to-Live as a universal bond
4. The origin of the Will-to-Live
5. An important ingredient: the VQ.

1. What is the Will-to-Live?

Our existence takes the form of a project that we have called the PTL. For every project there is necessarily an *intent* that provides a meaning to the project and accounts for all the efforts that will be made to ensure its implementation.

In the case of the PTL, we have stated that the purpose (or intent) that underlies it and explains it is our Will-to-Live.

Our contention is that our Will-to-Live is the very essence of our being. It is what gives sense not only to everything that we do or feel but also to the world as a whole and as we are able to perceive it.

The more we become aware of our Will-to-Live as the basic drive behind our emotions and actions, the better chance we will have of coping with our own lives and entertain a meaningful relationship with others.

My Will-to-Live is the essence of my Project-to-Live. It is what defines me in my very being and what determines me in all aspects of my behaviour.

'To live is to want to live, and no more!'

Now, stop here for a minute and react to the sentence above:

- What was your very first reaction when you read it?

- What is that reaction telling you about yourself?

- What would you have said instead?

So let's proceed.

The intent of my Project-to-Live, in other words my Will-to-Live, is to persevere in its very being, to preserve itself as such.

Hence my Project-to-Live is both reflexive and continuous:

> **Reflexive** in so far as it is entirely orientated towards itself and does not aim for any objective outside of itself. (This does not imply that it is indifferent to others.)

> **Continuous** in the sense that it never ceases to accomplish itself nor does it ever reach completion. Because the sole purpose of my Project-to-Live is the perpetuation of my Will-to-Live, I can say that it succeeds in its accomplishment as long as I remain alive, i.e. at every moment of my existence. But my Project-to-Live cannot,

by definition, ever cease, since its purpose is instead to always ensure its continuation. Only my death can interrupt it, although not thereby completing it. We shall see further on in what way this paradoxical condition of a project, which is always being accomplished, but yet can never relax, reflects itself inevitably in the impressions that we feel as living beings.

Break time! Think about yourself and the people who are close to you and check it out: Isn't it true that we are so keen to live that we endure and accept a lot of pain and misery for the sake of staying alive? What do you say?

2. My Will-to-Live as the ultimate reference

My Will-to-Live is the most intimate perception that I have of myself. When I try to go down to the deepest roots of my being (as deep as my awareness of my own self can take me) what I become aware of is this compelling desire to remain alive, to go on with my life.

When I ask myself what it is that drives me at the very bottom of my most intimate being, the answer that comes up is: my Will-to-Live.

My Will-to-Live is the very ultimate reference that I can use to explain what I think about things, what I do and what I feel. At the end of the day, everything that I perceive takes a meaning for me in the way that it responds to my Will-to-Live.

Of course this relation of meaning is not always discovered right away, nor is it obvious. We often satisfy ourselves with explanations that are tied to more immediate (intermediary references) causes. However, we shall see as we advance in this book that when we dig deeper (and deep enough) we inevitably come up with an ultimate understanding that refers one way or the other to our Will-to-Live.

The Will-to-Live is the ultimate reference for all living beings! I am what drives me, or I am my Will-to-Live.

Stop again, please. This deserves another pause. May we suggest that you close the book for a few minutes and just let your mind wander around the idea of the Will-to-Live as the foundation of your life.

3. The Will-to-Live as a universal bond

Our Will-to-Live is also what creates a bond between us all as living beings. It seems that we recognise the same compelling desire as the motive that drives others, and we understand that this very essence is what we have in common, in spite of all the possible differences that keep us apart.

It is also a fact that we even feel this solidarity, although to a lesser extent, with all the other non-human living beings which, just like us, are inexorably driven by their Will-to-Live.

Question

Do you accept the idea that:

- Plants also have a 'Will-to-Live';

- Animals will go all the way to stay alive;

- Human beings share the Will-to-Live with all other species?

4. The origin of the Will-to-Live

Obviously, when reading all that we have written above, the question that comes to mind is, how does this Will-to-Live come into existence? How does inert matter take the form of a live entity that tends to perpetuate itself as such?

As you can imagine, this is a 'big' question.

We believe that the rational answer to this matter is for science to provide. At what point in time did life appear? How does a certain conjunction of matter suddenly gel, so to speak, in a way that renders it self-preserving? What is the minimum nucleus of molecules, the necessary configuration of cells that results in the appearance of life as an autonomous force, driven by its own will?

There is a good chance that research will one day reveal the answers to this scientific riddle. Science is the answer to the above questions.

Meanwhile, the issue for us in this book is not so much to solve this technical question as to build up our awareness of the Will-to-Live itself as key to our understanding of the world and the motor of our existence.

There may remain for some readers, however, a basic question which can be formulated as follows:

- Why begin our reflection with the notion of our Will-to-Live?

- Why consider the Will-to-Live as the ultimate given from which all the rest stems?

- Is there nothing beyond this notion or another *intention* that accounts for it?

- Is there yet another transcending reference of meaning to which we can and should relate our Will-to-Live?

Our answer to that question is that our Will-to-Live is indeed the deepest reference that we can effectively perceive. Anything beyond that notion is no longer a matter of experience, but of speculation or belief! At least, that is so at this point in time in our evolution.

Whether or not there exists (upstream of our Will-to-Live) a cause or first intention, other than purely natural, that has designed us as a PTL is something that cannot be physically felt, measured or proven. It can only be decided on a private basis as a matter of faith. Since this book is not about faith but about reason, we shall limit ourselves to the Will-to-Live itself as the ultimate reference – a reference that can be universally related to, without precluding the possibility, for anyone who chooses to do so, to consider the Will-to-Live as the creation of a higher entity.

Stop again here. This is a heavy issue (especially for the true believers). So take some time to ponder on the following questions:

1. Is 'God' your ultimate reference?

2. Do you accept the idea that 'God' is a transcendent (beyond us) reference?

3. Do you see any incompatibility between the notion of 'God' and our concept of the Will-to-Live?

Ready to move on?

The basic drive that defines and determines me takes the form of a desire. Behind all my actions and feelings there is a compelling call for me to perpetuate my existence. All my other needs, whatever form they might take, derive from my primordial and insatiable desire to live.

This explains why we are never completely satisfied and why we always strive to go one step further in fulfilling our needs. Our desire to live can never end. One step can only lead to the next. Should we ever stop wanting, then we would indeed be dead.

It is true that we break up our lives into all sorts of sub-projects, which we tend each time to bring to completion. However, it is clear that all these sub-projects are but a means for us to keep in process our master project, which is our PTL (as we stated before!).

Whenever we satisfy one of our needs, we are just nourishing our main intention, which is the preservation and intensification of our life. As we have already said, whilst we aim for the completion of all our sub-projects, we need to be aware that there can be no end to our Project-to-Live.

As regards our PTL its end is all but its continuation as such.

The essence of our Project-to-Live lies in its intention or purpose. For me as an individual, this intention or purpose is no more than my Will-to-Live. My Will-to-Live is thus my essence as a living being as well as the essence of my Project-to-Live. *For this reason, when I speak of myself, of my Project-to-Live, or of my existence, I am always referring to the same thing, since all these terms cover one same essence, which is my Will-to-Live.*

While we all share the same essence, which is our Will-to-Live, we need to recognise however that it does not exist in every individual with the same intensity. For some reason, which again science is best appointed to discover, some people's drive to live is stronger than other people's.

Some people are more eager, hungrier, more impatient, more assertive, more insatiable than others. And there is a good chance that those who are driven by the more powerful compulsion will want to move more in order to ensure the accomplishment of their PTL.

5. An important ingredient: the VQ

Everybody can observe that highly entrepreneurial people, whatever their field of activity, are driven by a stronger than average Will-to-Live. They promote change, take risks, challenge systems and people.

There is no doubt that such people are pressed by a more

urgent and more compelling need to accomplish their PTL than other people working a more routine life.

Typically, one becomes an entrepreneur or a leader or a great achiever of some kind because one wants (needs) to, not by chance. And such a person strives and fights to achieve his/her goals, in the face of inevitable challenge and competition. Behind this attitude there is an appetite for life that is like a symptom of some kind of hyper-acuteness of one's Will-to-Live, or even perhaps of an extraordinary fear of not accomplishing duly one's PTL.

Anybody who has come close to a high achiever has felt these signs. It is useful to grasp what stands behind them to be able to interact with these people appropriately and not to be taken aback by behaviours on their part which seem exaggerated compared to what the ordinary person would do.

Those people have what we call a very strong VQ or *Vitality Quotient*.

The main factors that determine our VQ are:

1. Our innate personality, which is genetic and hardly possible to change.

2. The means that we dispose of to carry out our PTL, something that we shall develop in the next chapter. There is no doubt that the amount of potential that we can make use of as we face the challenge of accomplishing our PTL influences our VQ, which in turn stimulates our development and expansion. They act upon each other in a reciprocal way.

3. The existential events that we experienced in our life (education, training, professional situations, emotional experiences...).

Is it important to be aware of our VQ? We believe it is, for the following reasons:

Our VQ is the primary qualifier of our identity. It defines the degree to which we are motivated to accomplish our PTL, the drive that pushes us ahead and incites us to take initiative and action.

In an even more basic way of speech, one can say that our VQ designates our thirst, our greed of life. It's advisable therefore to be aware of our VQ, because it will more often than not give us the explanation of why we behave in one way or the other – for instance very passively, or hyper-actively – and also guide us when we need to decide on a course of action.

If our VQ is intrinsically low, it will be preferable to avoid aiming for overly ambitious goals, lest we risk missing them, and by repeatedly facing failures, end up weakening our VQ even more.

A relatively low VQ can also represent an important asset in anybody's life. It can provide the following (do you recognise yourself in this list?):

- A basic patience and controlled pace in dealing with the challenges of life.

- A greater tolerance for other people's ways of doing and feeling.

- A valuable capacity for soothing and appeasing highly strung people.

- An ability to put things into perspective and avoid impulsive decisions.

- A good control of the emotions.

On the other hand, if we are conscious of having a high VQ, we can easily give in to our desire to go for ever more challenging objectives, knowing that this is the form that our PTL is designed to take.

A high VQ can also be a source of problems because it can lead to the following (do you recognise yourself?):

- A rushed approach to dealing with matters and issues.

- A natural impatience with people.

- A tendency to want too much too quickly.

Similarly, it is valuable to properly assess the VQ of other people whom we deal with. We will have to adjust our demands or expectations of others to the degree to which we feel that they are able to face the challenge of life. We ought to know that people will not produce or achieve more than their Will-to-Live incites them to do so, but also that there is so to speak no limit to what can be expected from those whose Will-to-Live is insatiable.

Please be aware that in the second part of the book ('Tests and self-assessment exercises'), there is an instrument that will enable you to assess your own VQ. We encourage you to go through it before reading further.

We also suggest that you reflect on the people around you and assess their VQ:

- Who has a very strong VQ? How does it manifest itself? Is it good? Bad?

- Who has a very weak VQ? Why? How does it affect (positively or negatively) your relationship with that individual?

- Think about your children (if you have any) and have a good look at their VQ. How can you help them reinforce or beef up their VQ?

What are the leadership implications?

Here are three major leadership tips around the philosophical concept of the 'Will-to-Live':

1. Leading people by paying attention to their basic drive
2. Knowing your own VQ
3. Energising people and teams.

THE BASIC DRIVE

It is quite simple! Leaders must be able to answer anyone who asks the following question: *What's in it for me*? The answer is absolutely critical. To have an impact, it must have the following characteristics:

- Be clear and easy to grasp
- Be in line with the basic desires of the individual
- Credible (trust is the issue).

THE LEADER'S VQ

The questions leaders should address from time to time are:

- Is my VQ (energy level) in line with the requirements of the situation that I am in right now? Some situations require a very high VQ (a dramatic change, a new challenge, a crisis...). Some others can be better handled with a low VQ. (The situation is ambiguous and patience is in order; people are moving along and doing the right things...)

- How good am I at energising myself when needed? This is about the leader's flexibility and ability to mobilise him/herself quickly when appropriate. It seems that some leaders are stuck at a certain level of energy and unable to adjust it to differing environments (as well as people).

- Should I adjust my VQ to the expectations of my managers? Leaders should be careful when selling their ideas to their 'bosses'. They can either overdo it, understate it or get it just right. Their leadership behaviours can be perceived as too soft or overwhelming. To adjust the tone of the delivery in presenting ideas for decisions can be vital for organisational success.

ENERGISING PEOPLE AND TEAMS

Ten leadership guidelines on how to boost the VQ of the team members:

- Mobilise your people around an exciting vision
- Emphasise personal opportunities in the team action plan
- Behave as a energised role model
- Empower people
- Challenge people's ideas
- Use competition as a lever
- Play on people's self-esteem
- Allow for ambiguity
- Build on emotions
- Remove roadblocks.

Now, what you can do as a leader is to measure the energy level of your team. Here are some traits of a highly energised team (Where does your team stand regarding those indicators?):

- There's a lot of open discussion around
- Action is the name of the game
- Fast is better than slow
- People are actively involved
- Individual excitement is everywhere
- Unexpected questions are asked
- Ideas are challenged systematically
- Nobody is afraid of speaking up
- Winning is the name of the game
- Passion is obvious.

Let's make a dent in the universe!

Steve Jobs

5. The Power-to-Live: I am what I am capable of

What is it?

Everybody recognises that the notion of power is a determining factor in the implementation of our lives, not only at the individual level but also in our social interactions.

Actually we talk about power all the time, be it in politics ('superpowers', to be 'in power'), in business (power structure, empowerment, power games) or simply in terms of our capability to do something or of influencing other people, or still more commonly to buy something (purchasing power).

Although all these forms of power seem to carry different connotations, they all stem from the same basic concept, which is simply the power that we need and make use of to accomplish in one form or the other our Project-to-Live.

The purpose of this chapter is to clarify and dig into this concept of power.

We shall call the power dimension of our Project-to-Live, *the Power-to-Live*.

We will demonstrate how it constitutes an intrinsic part of our very being. We'll show that without a minimum of power we cannot live. We will find out how our power is actually composed, what the different ingredients are that make it up, how it is structured and how it allows us to exist and expand.

It short, we invite you to an exploration of what makes you be what you are and do what you do.

We shall also emphasise what we have mentioned already, which is that while we are similar with regard to the basic intent that pushes us to carry on – our Will-to-Live – we all rely on a specific personal composition of power to actually accomplish our PTL.

My use of power is what makes me different from you!

The Power-to-Live is a basic component of our identity... and certainly worth a chapter.

Stop (!) a second and make a list (yes, do pick up a pen, please) of what makes you different from some of the close people around you:

- Your family members
- Your friends
- Your colleagues at work
- Others.

Yes, there are differences. So the question now is to know where they are coming from. This is not a trivial question.

What's in it for me?

This section of the book will guide you in the exploration of what makes you unique and different from other people.

It will give you some pointers to understand better what makes your life what it is and where you should maybe go next. Even more crucially, it will assist you in putting what you are experiencing right now into perspective. Hopefully it will lead you to some 'good' personal decisions.

We also hope that this key chapter will demonstrate to you that life is rich, challenging, exciting and open to initiatives as well as expansion.

Rich because it is so diversified and so full of options and alternatives.

Challenging because it is not easy, as everybody knows, and can be extremely painful at times.

Exciting because it gives us a chance to be what we are and enjoy what we have.

As you will see, the PTL model is not a constraining and reductive one. Quite the opposite, in fact! Just look at the headings of the different sections of this chapter.

What is the red thread?

This chapter will address the following questions and issues:

1. Power: What for?
2. 'I am the world!'

3. The Power-to-Live, or the ammunition of life
4. We are running out of time
5. Fighting for the same 'pie'
6. Lost and yet alive.

1. Power: What for?

As mentioned in the introduction, our Power-to-Live is one of the three elements of the structure of our PTL (the other two being our Will-to-Live and our Way-to-Live).

As such, our Power-to-Live can be understood as being *the means by which our Will-to-Live can realise itself in the physical world of our existence.*

Our existence, in very general terms, as we experience it in our everyday life, is nothing else than the manifestation, in one form or the other, of our Power-to-Live. To have the power to do something always means, at the end of the day, to have the power to preserve and perpetuate our existence this way or the other.

My Power-to-Live, as its name indicates, is the means by which my Will-to-Live comes to realisation. Without it, my PTL is either asleep or dead.

Let us be careful here! My Power-to-Live is in no way in itself the accomplishment of my Project-to-Live, nor is it by the same token the finality of my project. For as we have said, my Will-to-Live realises itself only through its own perpetuation as such – as an intention, and not by reaching any kind of final goal.

And yet, my Power-to-Live and my Will-to-Live are interdependent and intimately linked, as my Power-to-Live derives its purpose from my Will-to-Live, and my Will-to-Live in turn depends on my Power-to-Live for its existence.

Finally, we should add that while the Will-to-Live, which is my essence, has the same aspect – although in different intensities – in all living beings, the very constituents of the Power-to-Live on the other hand vary in each individual.

It is what defines our identity and makes us what we are.

2. 'I am the world!'

Our Power-to-Live is composed of the totality of the things that constitute the world, *together* with the faculty that we have to activate them at our will.

Let us now explain what this perhaps disconcerting definition means.

Hardly anybody will dispute that the world is made of a combination of elements (objects, people and events) that are all eventually linked to one another through connections of causality and presumably other things that we still do not know anything about. So it looks as if any of these elements is likely to have an effect at one point in time, one way or the other, on the course of our existence.

In that sense, we can say that each and every element of the world is part of our Power-to-Live.

Considering also that our Power-to-Live, as we said before, is an intrinsic part of our PTL, we can conclude that *our identity as a living being is no other than the world as a whole.*

I am the world, and the world in its totality contributes to the accomplishment of my PTL.

Let's say it again: 'I am the world.'

Hold it right there! Please react to the statement just above:

- Do you accept it?

- Do you reject it?

- Does it shock you?

On the other hand, however, our Power-to-Live only exists to the extent that all those elements which constitute our environment, when taken together, favourably affect our PTL.

In other words, it is not enough to merely draw an inventory of all the components of the world in just one mass. It wouldn't make sense, because then the same inventory would apply to identify all the different individuals living on this earth, and there would exist only one single identity, the same for all, which is absurd.

In fact, my Power-to-Live depends not only on the sheer existence of the things of the world but also on their actual positioning as well as on their order of arrangement as it relates to me in my body, at the core of my physical existence.

My capacity to benefit from my environment so that it favours my life is absolutely critical. So I must make sure (as much as possible) that all the elements of that environment are interconnected and converge through causal links towards the nucleus of my PTL, which we have identified as being my Will-to-Live.

It behoves me as a living being to constantly act upon this arrangement in such a way that it becomes always more favourable to me.

It is up to me to make sure that the causal chaining of the events of the world contributes in the best possible way to the realisation of my PTL.

Let us say it once more: My personal Power-to-Live, and hence my identity, is made up of the totality of the elements of the world in their particular order of arrangement as seen from the perspective of the vital core of my person.

Thus my Power-to-Live offers itself as a purposeful instrument, in the sense that all its components are logically tied together and that the whole is connected to one single and constant intention which is the perpetuation of my existence.

This instrument of course is composed, at every given moment, of objects, people and events, some of which are favourable to me whilst others are not. I nevertheless call it my Power-to-Live because as a whole it is favourable to my PTL; for clearly, if it were not, I would not be alive.

For us as individuals, our first effort should be to represent ourselves in the full measure of what we are – that is to say, the world as a whole. We must see ourselves through the world...

We are used to identifying ourselves with our *person*, which we generally regard as being our body, our mind (which we often consider as somewhat separate from our physical body) and, for some, our soul. Rarely do we see ourselves as extending beyond those limits.

Yet do we not constantly make use of many aspects of what we wrongly call our 'environment' to conduct our existence? Are there not many things or people that benefit us, which contribute to our PTL? Why do we then not include them in the definition of what/who we are?

In fact, as we shall see below, we are composed of layers of power which all make up our identity as living beings and which extend far beyond our body and mind, to potentially include the whole world (as we claimed before).

Let us therefore try to envision ourselves as an unlimited extension of objects and events, all converging towards our Will-to-Live. This Will-to-Live in turn produces a constant impulse to arrange these objects and events in an order that is always more favourable to our PTL. It is a process. It is dynamic and dialectic, in the sense that one impacts the other and vice versa.

Adopting this perspective implies that we become part of the world in its totality. No man is an island.

Anything that occurs in the world occurs to me and anything that I do will impact the world as a whole. 'And therefore never send to know for whom the bell tolls,' said the poet, John Donne, 'it tolls for thee.'

There is no such thing as escape or withdrawal: these attitudes just indicate a change of position within a world that inevitably remains ours and our selves. This understanding should encourage us to accept our engagement in the world wholeheartedly and manage our lives accordingly. The world is mine, the world is I and it behoves me to try *to make it become what I would like it to be.*

Let's work now on some illustrations of the statement 'I am the world':

ILLUSTRATIONS

Here are some examples to illustrate what we mean by 'I am the world', showing how any object/person in the world is liable to affect my PTL and is therefore part of *me* as a living being.

Some things affect me *passively,* i.e. contribute to my PTL without having been intentionally triggered by me:

- The sun that casts light and heat upon the world

- The air that I can breathe

- My body that functions in part automatically so as to preserve itself and remain alive

- My parents and friends who love me

Other things I can influence or *master* so that they favour my PTL:

- My skills

- My health (to some extent)

- Many different people that I can influence
- My property, which I can make use of.

3. The Power-to-Live, or the ammunition of life

Our Power-to-Live, as we have just mentioned, is determined by the way that the things that make up the world are located, interconnected and converge towards us, and by our ability to trigger them so that they react in our favour.

The categories of my Power-to-Live that we will now review reflect the typical arrangements following which the elements of the world are submitted to my Will-to-Live.

It is important to underline again (at the risk of boring you, the reader) that as individuals we differ from one another precisely by the way that we integrate all these various arrangements in the construction of our personal Powers-to-Live.

Again, think about it:

- How do you approach the world?

- What makes you unique in your personal grasp of the world?

- How aware are you of your special ways of looking at things and people?

Now let us proceed with the analysis of the different layers of power that typically make up our Power-to-Live:

- My *person*: this is the core of my identity. It includes my body, my mind, my aptitudes and traits of character, my health (and for some, my soul). It is the centre of my personality and what makes me what I am. It is the word (concept?) used by us to define the centre of the person or the 'gestalt' where all the pieces fall together to constitute what we are. Actually, my *personality* reflects the specific way by which my self undertakes to implement my PTL, given the intrinsic qualities of my body, my mind, my character and aptitudes and my health.

- My *body* is the condition of both my essence (my Will-to-

Live) and my existence. It is through my body that my
Will-to-Live comes to existence but it is also my body that
maintains my Will-to-Live in its state of intention, as the
will of its own perpetuation. Thus my body is the minimal
nucleus of my Power-to-Live, indispensable to its existence and to its expansion in the world.

My body is the part of the world that is the most completely
devoted to the accomplishment of my PTL. It presents itself as a
system of interdependent elements, each one of which tends to
the preservation of the whole. It is because it is so exclusively
and evidently dedicated to my PTL, and is at the same time the
minimal condition of its existence, that my body is generally
assimilated to my very identity as a living being.

And yet my body is no more stable in its existence or clearly
defined in its limits or contours than any other component of my
Power-to-Live. My body does in fact change at every instant in its
appearance and its constitution. It carries the marks of its
experience of life and time.

Is my body the same at two separate moments of my existence, or when an accident or a disease deprives me of one of
my organs? To such a question one can answer yes or no. No, if
I have changed in my appearance or in my ability to act: how
could I pretend to be the same if I cannot behave as I used to, if
for instance I have lost an arm or a leg? And yet, I cannot avoid
answering positively in so far as my body, in spite of all its
transformations, has somewhere maintained its capacity to
preserve at least the essence of its being, i.e. its Will-to-Live.

Therefore one can recognise that there is something like a
hierarchical order in the components of my body, given that
there exists this irreducible organic structure without which the
whole of my PTL could not persist as such. As was said earlier,
we do not know exactly what are the limits, the contents or the
physical conditions of existence of this minimal biological
structure, although science might be able to discover them one
day.

As for the questions pertaining to its possible purpose or
meaning, we shall not try to answer them in this book, since we
have defined the Will-to-Live as the *ultimate rational foundation*
of meaning which can be experienced; a foundation which of

course cannot itself be founded, since it would lead us to look for yet another foundation to relate it to, and so on for ever.

My body is also the place from which is initiated the implementation of my PTL. It is in the kernel of this organic structure that lie the controls of my Power-to-Live. It is from and through my body that I will strive throughout my existence to change the arrangement of the elements of the world in a way that my body again will evaluate as being the most favourable to my PTL. It is therefore also at the level of my body that I will determine and manifest my Way-to-Live, my behaviour, in all its different aspects, as we shall review later on.

- My *mind* is a faculty that is part of my physical organism. It allows me to reflect on my PTL, or to be more precise, it allows my PTL to reflect itself, so as to orientate my conscious activity in a way that is always the most favourable to my PTL. It includes essential elements such as my abilities to:

  - Reason

  - Dream

  - Probe and explore

  - Assess and measure

  - Organise and create order

  - Orient myself and decide

  - Speculate and guess

  - Memorise and remember

  - Create and invent

  - Change and modify

  - Feel and vibrate

  - Energise.

- My *health* is the state of my body and its faculty to contribute to my PTL. The attention I pay to my health generates:

  - My concern about my diet

  - My ways of handling sickness

- My physical activities (sports...)
- My desire to rest.

All these behaviours reflect the importance that I attribute to my health as my physical ability to continue to accomplish my PTL.

- My character and aptitudes
  - My ability to learn
  - My capacity to reproduce
  - My disposition towards love
  - My motivation
  - My imagination and creativity
  - My stamina (or energy, as we saw in Chapter 4)
  - My temper
  - My ability to lead, communicate with and motivate others.

- My *relatives.* They are the people that I tend to assimilate to myself because their existence is a way of extension of my own person.

For instance, I will strongly identify with my children. Since they originate in my own body, I would generally consider them as being an extension of my personal PTL. In the same way, I will typically (but of course not necessarily) be inclined to assimilate my parents' existence to my own, and consider that what affects them affects me no differently. Here, the cause for this is again the kinship of bodies, but seen this time from a reversed perspective.

A similar tendency will be observed with regard to all my blood relationships, although it may well diminish as the degree of kinship gets weaker and weaker.

This assimilation of other PTLs to my own, however, is not limited only to the human beings with which I share a blood relationship. It is part of my human nature to recognise in my fellow human a Project-to-Live which is (I believe) identical to my own and therefore to feel, through a simple transfer effect, the concern that the other person may have about the accomplishment of her personal PTL. This identification will induce me to feel for her and to want to contribute, to an extent that we shall have to define further on, to her success. We shall come back to this important issue, since it constitutes the basis for our moral conduct in life.

- My *education* means in this instance all my mental build-up in the broadest sense, in which I include my knowledge (my representation of the world) and my skills. We should maybe single out:
  - My acquired professional capabilities
  - My people skills
  - My good manners.

- My *property* is everything that is recognised legally or *de facto* as belonging to me and that I can dispose of as I wish. To my private property, I shall add the natural elements such as the sun or air or the sight of a landscape. I own them together with my fellow humans, and I am free to enjoy them, as long as their use is not subject to any legal or enforced constraint (in which case we are drawn back to the preceding category).

- My *conventional ties* are the agreements that I make with other people whose PTL are in competition with my own. Through them we decide to distribute between us a part of our respective Powers-to-Live in proportion to our already existing status of power and with the view of serving our mutual interests. There exists a multitude of such agreements, running from simple verbal deals to all sorts of transactions, purchases, sales, insurance policies, employment contracts, by-laws, laws, constitutions etc.

- My *reputation* (or *prestige* or *glory*) represents an advantage for me, as it reflects that others recognise my value for them and that I can thus expect that they will be willing in exchange to favour my own PTL.

- My *influence* reflects the way that I can control the behaviour of others by making use of my force (in which case my influence becomes constraining) or my capacity to persuade or my authority. The latter is natural, inherent to my temperament or resulting from my social or hierarchical position, including possible conventional agreements.

- My *freedom* is to be understood here as my physical capacity to do what I want. As such it is clearly a part of my Power-to-Live since it appears as the condition of my ability to exercise it.

- My *means of entertainment* are the resources that I have access to (art, sports, books, gardening etc.) when I want to stimulate my faculties and intensify my impression of being alive. They are part of my Power-to-Live, since they open the possibility of at least having the illusion that I am contributing, by entertaining myself, to the accomplishment of my PTL.

- *Chance* is probably one of the most influential categories of my Power-to-Live. By chance we mean all the events that can affect our PTL but which we see as unpredictable and/or independent of any identifiable intention. Things just happen all the time that can do me good or bad. As such they enter into my Power-to-Live: if I am lucky, this represents an increase in my Power-to-Live, if I am unlucky it is just the opposite. This is another way of showing that I can never be exactly aware of the measure of my Power-to-Live.

- My *salvation* constitutes the Power-to-Live that I am banking on to perpetuate my PTL in the other world, to the extent of course that I believe in the possibility of such a supernatural prolongation of my existence.

RECAP: The categories of our Power-to-Live

- **My Person:** my body, my mind, my personality, my health
- **My Relatives:** my family, my friends, my associates
- **My Education:** my knowledge, my skills, my manners
- **My Property:** my belongings, my money
- **My Ties:** my contracts, my commitments
- **My Influence:** my authority, my ascendance, my charm, my charisma

- **My Means of Entertainment:** my capacity to buy or have access to sources of entertainment, sports, books, arts, etc.

- **My Freedom:** my liberty to move, to access public areas

- **My Luck:** my situation with regard to the unpredictable events that my affect me

- **My Salvation:** my 'life' in the other world.

Each person, each one of us is different in the way that we build up our individual Power-to-Live. Following our innate characteristics, our upbringing, the environment in which we live and our life experience in general, we organise our Power-to-Live in the way that we believe is the most suitable and also the most accessible to us. Some of us will tend to bank on their physical aspect or their charm to get the most out of life; others will count on their education, still others will run for the money, or for political power or hierarchical authority, or even gamble. Each person will decide according to the equation of their being and of their situation in life what it is that they need to work on most to enhance their chances of accomplishing their PTL.

It is important that I learn to know myself well in terms of how my Power-to-Live is organised:

- Which aspects of my Power-to-Live do I chiefly rely on to accomplish my PTL?

- Which ones do I feel are the strongest, so that I can lean on them in order to expand?

- Which ones are the weakest, so that I can work on them and develop them?

Similarly, I must learn to evaluate the Powers-to-Live of the people that I deal with, so that I can relate to them with a better knowledge of what their strengths and weaknesses are, but also of what sectors of their Power-to-Live they are attempting to develop or give priority to. This will help me to become aware of what they value most and allow me to adjust my behaviour towards them accordingly.

Let's have a break here and work (if you do not mind – and if you do, just ignore this part and move on to the next chapter!).

The question we would like to address now is, do you know your Power-to-Live?

The following assessment will help you to establish your personal Power Map, as you understand it today.

Personal assessment

Going back to the list repeated below, try to identify which ones of these categories of your Power-to-Live you tend to favour when you manage your existence, and put them in a ranking order. If you feel that there are categories that are missing from the list, add them in.

- **My Person**: my body, my mind, my personality, my health

- **My Relatives**: my family, my friends, my associates

- **My Education**: my knowledge, my skills, my manners

- **My Property**: my belongings, my money

- **My Ties**: my contracts, my commitments

- **My Influence**: my authority, my ascendance, my charm, my charisma

- **My Means of Entertainment**: my capacity to buy or have access to sources of entertainment, sports, books, arts, etc.

- **My Freedom**: my liberty to move, to access public areas

- **My Luck**: my situation with regard to the unpredictable events that my affect me

- **My Salvation**: my 'life' in the other world.

Now reflect on the following questions:

Do you feel that you are effectively making use, in carrying out your existence in your private life or at work, of the categories of your Power Map that you favour? Do your current activities give you a chance to develop those components of your Power-to-Live that you give priority to? If not, what do you intend to do about it?

4. We are running out of time

Any project, in so far as it is an intention turned towards the future, develops through *time*. The situation is no different with our Project-to-Live.

In addition, our PTL offers this particularity that it aims for nothing else than its own perpetuation in time. Therefore, the more our PTL is apt to extend itself through time, the more it is able to achieve its purpose.

The time that we can dispose of to live is thus another measure of our capacity to accomplish our PTL. Time is thus another way for us to express our Power-to-Live. No one knows exactly how much time he or she disposes of to continue to extend her PTL, but each one of us nevertheless has an intimate intuition that he or she integrates spontaneously as another representation of the Power-to-Live.

Thus we all feel that our time to live is limited and that as we grow older we progressively lose an essential part of our Power-to-Live, even though any other of its components may possibly increase.

We also have this painful impression of an irreversible loss when we believe that we have wasted our time, instead of devoting it to strengthening the chances of accomplishment of our PTL.

This is not to say that time – duration – is the only measure of the accomplishment of our PTL, and that all we ever look for is to survive as long as possible.

Obviously there is another vital measure of the realisation of our PTL which is the *intensity* with which we live.

We want to underline here that even when the intensity of our life is to be taken into account as a measure of accomplishment, time still remains the ultimate condition of this accomplishment. We must realise that without time there can be no intensity of life at all, and whatever (positive) intensity we might reach in our lives, we will want it to last for as much time as possible.

But by the same token, we have also learned to take advantage of all that makes us different, and to exploit this diversity to make use collectively of all the various ways by which we can preserve and expand our existences.

5. Fighting for the same 'pie'

If it is true that:

1. We spend the major part of our life working on the order of arrangement of the things that make up the world so as to render it more favourable to our personal PTL, and

2. Every other living being on earth is striving towards the same objective...

Then it is easy to understand that all these simultaneous PTLs are, by nature, in conflict.

The coexistence in the world of living beings is thus by essence conflictual. This results in a state of tension, which reflects, at any given moment, the existing relations of strength or, to put it in our now familiar words, of the PTLs in competition.

One does not need to look any further for the explanation of all the fights, battles and wars that have been tearing and keeping people apart ever since mankind's existence. This is a given that goes with the fact that there is only one world and billions of living beings are struggling to mould it into a shape that suits their respective Projects-to-Live.

Obviously as we organise ourselves socially we are able to alleviate this potential conflict to the maximum extent possible, but this can only be the outcome of a cultural effort to attenuate the natural conflicting coexistence of PTLs as stated above.

All through this book we shall learn to evolve in this dual relationship with the other, which is inherent to the structure of our being. The others are my brothers/sisters in the way that they share the same essence as myself, which is their Will-to-Live. But the others are also intrinsically different from me in the capacity that they have to make use of or to carry out their Projects-to-Live.

This tension between what we all have in common and what makes us all different accounts for the complicated relationships that human beings entertain. We cannot avoid solidarity, understanding the deep aspirations of our fellow beings, feeling empathy and compassion (or, on the contrary, fear, despise or even hate them when they go against our or other people's – that we identify with – predominant Will-to-Live). At the same time we are always surprised, both attracted and turned away by the means through which others undertake to conduct their existences and which differ from our own.

To overcome this tension we have established through time transcending values such as love and respect for the other person. Those values acknowledge our common essence and remind us of its precedence when we tend to forget it because of our differences; from such values we derive guidelines of conduct which we refer to as moral behaviour.

As I become aware of the necessity to accomplish my PTL, I cannot help but to perceive every other living being on this earth as a potential threat. All the living organisms are engaged in the same struggle to perpetuate their own existence, which implies striving to change the arrangement of things and events so that they contribute to their own PTL.

There is always a good chance that what the other wants will to some extent conflict with what I want, so that we shall end up with opposed interests. Hence the most immediate feelings that people have for one another before entering into a more constructive relationship, and which take the forms of suspicion, fear, antagonism and aggressiveness.

Luckily, living beings and particularly humans have learnt that there are ways to turn this potential conflict into forms of relations that are more beneficial to the PTL of all parties involved.

By banking on the interests that they have in common, people and societies have developed means of mutual assistance and cooperation that alleviate the inherent tension between us all and give way to feelings of trust, respect and love.

We are nevertheless constantly reminded that closely behind these fragile positive feelings there always lurks the perception of the other as being a competitor in our struggle for life. It doesn't take much for this brutal reality to take over and generate a less cooperative behaviour on the part of the parties involved.

It seems then that I constantly live with an ambiguous perception of my fellow human. He is my brother, as we share the same Will-to-Live; but he is also my foe, since he is living off the same world as myself.

She is my partner, as we cooperate to transform the world in a way that suits our mutual interest; but she is my competitor who is always likely to take advantage of the breaks that I might give her.

I love him, but I am ready to hate him. I trust her, but I could easily become suspicious of her. I am ready to put my life into his hands, but I also fear that he could kill me if he needed to.

Such are the contradictory feelings that we entertain towards each other and which, in spite of all the precepts that we have developed to regulate them, remain very unstable and likely to shift with the course of events.

'I shall help you if I can, I shall kill you if I must, I shall kill you if I can, I shall help you if I must,' sang Leonard Cohen.

Question

Can you recognise the dual tension (cooperation versus competition) in yourself and your close environment? Take your spouse (or boyfriend/girlfriend) and identify what:

- You share in common (interests, values, expectations etc.)

- You disagree on

- You give to each other

- You do to solve conflicting interests

- You have given up...

6. Lost and yet alive

The review of the structure of our Power-to-Live has underlined that our identity as living beings extends itself well beyond what we are used to consider as our person, our mere self.

Although it is true that my physical organism is the place where the most evident part of my Power-to-Live is located, this does not preclude the fact that my Power-to-Live also includes my environment (as opposed to just my body), which is also part of me in the sense that through each one of its elements it exerts a more or less discernable and significant influence on my PTL.

This leads us to the following paradoxical conclusion. Considering that: (i) I am unable to grasp where it is that my Power-to-Live really begins; (ii) I am not capable of circumscribing the world in its totality; (iii) the world, including my very body, is in constant transformation, meaning that my Power-to-Live never remains the same ...then I have to conclude and accept that as a living being I can never know myself in an adequate fashion, so that the only part of the structure of my PTL with which I can identify in an unmistakable and permanent way is my essence, which is no other than my Will-to-Live.

As an individual, I live with an ambiguous perception of myself. To be wise is to be confused!

On the one hand, there is no doubt that I feel a sense of permanence in my identity, the fact that day after day I am the same person, whatever may happen to me and however I may change physically, mentally and in my situation.

This reference of stability that I have is my PTL itself, the idea that I want to carry on with my existence, the consciousness that my project has a past, a present and a projected future.

On the other hand, however, I have the impression that I am changing all the time, maybe growing stronger, maybe weaker, winning here, losing there, and also inevitably that time is running out, that I am getting older every day, so that finally I am never really the same person.

To that one can add the feeling of uncertainty that goes with the awareness that we never really know what our Power-to-Live is, since it includes all the potential events of the world that can one way or the other affect us, while we never precisely know how or when.

So as an individual I have to cope with this tension and uncertainty.

I shall find comfort in the permanence of my Will-to-Live, and shelter more mixed feelings as I consider my Power-to-Live. The instability and lack of clarity of my Power-to-Live will generate an impression of excitement, stimulation and challenge when I think of all the opportunities I have of expanding and securing my PTL. It will also trigger in most cases a feeling of discomfort and anxiety, especially when I realise the uncertainty of the means that I can make use of to perpetuate my existence.

We believe that it can only do us good to understand all these implications about the way that we are intrinsically made because the clearer the causes of our well-being or ill-being, the better chances we have of integrating their effects and also hopefully mastering them.

We recommend to the reader to stop here and just go (if you have not done it yet as suggested at the end of the first chapter) to the part on 'Tests and self-assessment exercises' to take the test on ambiguity. If you have done it, it is not a bad idea to revisit it. How good are you at taking advantage of uncertainty?

What are the leadership implications?

Let's examine what we call the 'PTL leadership way'. It consists in:

1. Knowing what the *major Power Map ingredients* are for each team member or even business partner. The questions that can be asked are:

    -   What makes that individual click?

    -   What does he or she care about?

    -   What is it that he or she talks about all the time?

    -   What triggers strong reactions (positive or negative) in that individual?

    -   What makes that person very happy (unhappy)?

    -   What are the colleagues saying about him or her?

    -   What is non-verbal behaviour saying about his or her moods?

2. *Ranking the Power Map elements of your team members* so that you know what the three major ones are. Then you as a leader can:

    -   Show the team member that you know and understand what he or she cares about;

    -   Design the jobs around the individuals' Power Maps (as much as possible); and

    -   Build the team spirit around the shared aspirations.

3. Managing the team and organisational environment so that people get a chance to stretch themselves and *expand their Power Maps*.

    -   Give the team members new challenges

    -   Encourage them to explore new avenues

    -   Provide the proper incentives (What's in it for me?) for personal discoveries and development.

Needless to say, the best way for leaders to accomplish the above is to do it in cooperation – face to face – with the team members. Sometimes it is also possible (recommended, even) to use the process of the Power Map inventory as a team-building exercise.

Activity is the only reality.

Novalis

6. The Way-to-Live: I am what I do...

What is it?

What I do... This is about the third element of the Project-to-Live model. Remember:

- First component: the Will-to-Live (the basic drive that we share in common with all living beings: 'To live is to want to live').

- Second component: the Power-to-Live (all the means that we use in our unique way to ensure the perpetuation of our life: 'I am the world'). And now,

- Third component: the Way-to-Live!

My Way-to-Live consists in activating my Power-to-Live which, until now, we have only considered as a means or a potential. In other words, my Way-to-Live represents the dynamic part of my Project-to-Live.

It is through my behaviour that I can change the disposition of the world, as I strive to make it always more favourable to my Project-to-Live.

By my behaviour, I thus imply the totality of the manifestations of my Power-to-Live, as it activates its potentialities.

Or, to put it differently, given that my life develops through time, I can define my behaviour as the sum of the events that constitute the implementation of my Project-to-Live during the whole duration of my existence.

Stop! Please read the above sentence again. What does it mean for you?

My behaviour is an essential part of the structure of my Project-to-Live, one without which it could not accomplish itself. It derives its purpose from the existence of the other parts of that structure which, in turn, without it would lose all meaning.

As an integral part of my Project-to-Live, my behaviour, is thus also a principal component of my identity: it is through my behaviour that my existence manifests itself. Without it, the PTL is just a metaphor or a wishful thought!

What's in it for me?

You are going to get a chance to look at some key dimensions of your own behaviours or actions.

You will see what the main 'strategies' to enhance your Power-to-Live are and analyse some alternatives to the activation and expansion of your vital functions.

Again, you will be (perhaps) shocked and perplexed. The idea is to make you look at your life from a new and fresh perspective. Hopefully it will help you rethink what you do with your life and examine some personal options (what else could you do?).

The question we are going to raise in this first chapter about our Way-to-Live is, 'Why do you do what you do?'

What is the red thread?

The main questions and issues that we will review are:

1. Why do I behave the way I do?
2. What is work after all, and who needs it?
3. Anything wrong with doing nothing?
4. Is there an alternative to work?
5. Where do I go from here?

1. Why do I behave the way I do?

We will be using the word 'behaviour' in its very basic sense, i.e. any fashion by which we manifest our existence, be it through actions or emotions.

The questions that come up are: 'How come we act in such a way in such given circumstances? Why do we do this and not something else? Why will the other person react in a different way? Is there some kind of common denominator behind these different ways of behaving, in spite of the fact that they may indeed be quite contrasted and even contradictory?'

In fact, what we need to know at this stage is that what lies in the background of our behaviour in all circumstances is our

PTL, our Will-to-Live, which will in every case motivate our decisions and the actions that follow.

To do is always necessarily to do what we believe at that moment is best for our PTL!

2. What is work after all, and who needs it?

According to us, *work* is the fundamental piece of our behaviour – that is to say, of the way we carry out our PTL.

However, you must realise that we are not using the word 'work' in its common sense, i.e. work as being assimilated to labour or to a job. Here is our proposed definition:

Work is the process by which we activate our vital functions and/or any other element of our Power-to-Live. It is everything we do to ensure the conservation and the growth of our Power-to-Live.

We work when we make use of any of the elements of our Power Map to accomplish our PTL.

Hold it! Have you ever looked at work this way? Think again: 'To work is to activate my Power-to-Live!'

It is quite clear of course, in that sense, that to have a job or an occupation is also a part (a very important one, in many cases) of the PTL.

Work, therefore, is the most essential manifestation of our life. Without work (according to our definition), we get stale and atrophy and eventually die!

Let's say it again: 'By work we refer to all the acts by which we intend to contribute to the preservation and/or enhancement of our Power-to-Live.'

In this context we are not afraid of stating that 'Work is life' and that 'To live is to work'. Let us explain what we mean by that.

Below is a list of the most current actions that we can categorise as work:

1. Eating
2. Drinking
3. Dressing
4. Exercising
5. Learning and educating ourselves

6. Establishing and maintaining social relations

7. Creating, inventing, innovating

8. Earning a living

9. Travelling and discovering...

10. ...and many others.

In short, through our work we testify to our existence and expand our options. We also strengthen our potential to live.

What we are saying is that all the tasks that we perform (with or without pleasure) belong to work.

Not to work is not to be alive.

We must point out that to consider work as an evil is to consider life as a nuisance and is therefore extremely dangerous for our survival. It is also obvious that to minimise the pain while working (our definition) is natural and healthy.

So, yes, we need work. Everybody does! The question is, 'How can we make the process of working effective and pleasant?' Or, even more important, 'How can I make work more meaningful for myself?'

Being in charge of my own life (more about this later), I must accept the idea that each time I undertake any kind of action, my underlying purpose is the perpetuation and consolidation of my PTL.

Everything I do affects in one way or another my Project-to-Live.

Not only are we looking after the maximum return on our actions for the sake of our PTL but also for the greatest possible pleasure. We work to live and to enjoy.

To act lightly or frivolously, without enough reflection, is to treat our PTL in a poor and dangerous way.

One more word on work: what we do at work (we are talking now about the restricted sense of the word, i.e. about the job that we have) is obviously a big part of our Way-to-Live, and it does impact our PTL in a tremendous way. There is no question that a satisfying job will mean (in most cases) that:

1. We are using some of our vital functions and capacities.

2. We are expanding our Power-to-Live through our job.

3. We are in line with the main purpose of our life (i.e. its perpetuation).

To manage our lives is basically to make sure that a maximum of our vital functions (as we got them from nature, education, social experiences...) are fully used as well as developed.

It is also a question of acquiring new ones to widen our chances to be (live) and grow.

3. Anything wrong with doing nothing?

If we do nothing and do it for quite some time, something quite dramatic (or dangerous) then happens to us.

To do nothing in order to rest and get our energy back is one thing. To do nothing as a way of life is a waste and can be very irresponsible indeed. By doing nothing useful, we just consume our existing Power-to-Live to remain alive, and eventually this potential will melt away and we will no longer be able to go on. Don't forget that work is the way by which we preserve and maintain our ability to carry on!

This danger, luckily enough, will be signalled to us by a specific mechanism of our PTL. In many cases, in fact, the absence of action will lead to a negative impression that we call *boredom*.

Boredom is an impression (more about impressions, feelings and emotions in the next chapter) that seizes us when a given amount of the capacities that constitute our Power-to-Live are not (or not sufficiently) mobilised. We then become idle, or in other words, in contradiction with our very essence which is to live.

Boredom exists:

1. When the situations that we are in (at work, with family, friends...) do not give us a fair chance to use all of our vital functions opportunely;

2. When we are not able to get involved in anything exciting or worth the effort;

3. When a required action would cost us more to accomplish than it would yield in return.

Boredom is a negative impression loaded with discomfort and sometimes pain. To be bored is to have the impression that one is wasting something precious...

Think about the boredom that you experience when your mental functions are underused...

Think about what many organisations do to people when they give them minimal, non-challenging (boring) jobs instead of offering opportunities for full realisation and growth. People then experience a malfunction of their PTL. They are bored. They feel uneasy and look outside their work place for alternatives. Boredom is the sign of a gap between what we experience and what we need!

To keep busy and do things is to stay alive. Most people feel uneasy when they are not sufficiently occupied. All of a sudden they have the impression that something is wrong. They experience a malaise and even, in some cases, a guilty feeling.

This state of boredom can even lead to anxiety and depression. We have lost our purpose in life. We have lost touch with our very meaning, which is our PTL!

To be bored is very close to getting a first taste of dying, since our vital functions have been turned off and our Power-to-Live turned away from its primary function, which is to mobilise itself and to preserve and increase our capacity to live.

To increase our understanding of boredom we can observe that there are times when:

1. All our vital functions and our Power-to-Live are fully turned on and used. There is a good chance that we then feel exhilarated. These are special moments in our lives. Most people are always looking for a repeat of those privileged instances.

   – Question: Can you remember such a time?

2. Some parts of our Power Map are more important than others. Therefore the non-actualisation of those elements will quickly trigger some kind of boredom. Something essential for me is not present. I feel bored because what's happening is of no interest for me.

   – Question: Are you able to identify a situation that you found yourself in and which did not give you a fair chance to use some of your key functions? Try to turn back to the predominant categories of your Power Map as you identified them earlier.

3. It is inevitable that when we indulge in any particular task for a prolonged period of time a whole range of our functions remains unoccupied, and that can also be a

source of boredom. We need to be exposed to a certain variety of challenges or situations to have a fair chance to really tap most of our capacities and fulfil our key aspirations.

- Question: Have you ever worked with somebody who challenged you and gave you a chance to enlarge your Power Map?

It should also be noted that the more we are conscious of the totality of our vital functions (Power Map), the more chances there are that we will be sensitive to boredom. Because for such people who feel in touch with life through a wide range of their physical and mental capacities, there will be of course a greater need to keep them activated, lest they fall in idleness and thus generate an impression of boredom. We believe that artists, for example, are people who sense life in an exceptionally acute way, as if their whole person were in some way electrified and vibrating in its need to accomplish their PTL as completely as possible. For such people, no normal occupation will ever suffice to give them the feeling that they are living fully enough. That is why they will tend to recreate life artificially, so as to make it stimulating enough to occupy their vital functions as intensely as they need. A work of art is thus an intensified representation of life, a booster that the artist fabricates in order to feel that he is fully engaged in his/her PTL.

It could be said that people who claim that they never experience boredom are maybe those who are good at finding ways to keep themselves busy by all means and at any cost; or in some cases perhaps they fear boredom to the extent that they prefer not to recognise it when it's there!

Finally, boredom can be a signal suggesting to us that it may be time to explore our needs and expectations (our PTL) in a deeper way and discover what we should do next to move on with our lives and grow. In such cases, boredom can be seen as a useful feeling which will help us to adjust our Power Maps to the needs of our PTL.

It could be quite interesting for you, the reader, to take a minute and answer the following questions:

1. Are you ever bored?

2. What triggers boredom in you?
3. How do you cope with boredom?

4. Is there an alternative to work?

Yes, there is! And it is called *entertainment*. What is it?

Entertainment is an activity in which we indulge for the mere reason that it gives us the *impression* that our PTL is activated and running.

But watch out! Entertainment is really a subterfuge. It's a fake form of work. We think that we are doing something in line with our Project-to-Live. But we are not really.

It just seems that when we are not able to occupy our vital functions in a meaningful way (for some internal or external reasons), we switch to an artificial stimulation called 'entertainment'.

This happens when we dance, play, do sports, read, discuss, or just go into daydreaming for the sole purpose of keeping ourselves busy and happy. The major difference between work and entertainment is that the former is effectively enriching our Power-to-Live, whereas the latter is just creating an illusion of such a thing!

Entertainment does not actually enhance our Power-to-Live. It has another purpose of its own.

The main purpose of entertainment can be identified as a way to:

1. Keep us going when there is nothing meaningful to do, and in so doing avoid boredom;
2. Intensify our impression of being alive.

There is however some danger in getting too involved in entertainment. It takes away the time and energy that we need to use and enhance our real functions and Power-to-Live.

In other words, entertainment can by no means replace work. With entertainment there is no added value in terms of our Power-to-Live. We are literally wasting our time and our life. Entertainment is quite acceptable and even recommendable for a while since it provides pleasurable impression of living intensely; but it is counterproductive if carried on for too long, since it is only an illusion of work, and therefore of life!

A few remarks on the way entertainment functions:

1. Only the individual who is involved in some form of action can decide if what he or she does is work or entertainment: it depends on the intent with which the activity is undertaken, not on the form that it takes. The same activity, let's say a sport, for instance, can be indulged in either for the kicks (entertainment) or the output – health or fitness, for example (work).

2. No activity takes the form of pure work or pure entertainment. Very often we'll find a mixture of productive work and fun in all our human actions.

3. People who only entertain themselves and live for the fun of it, shrink and lose their ability to shine, grow and contribute. Very soon they have nothing to say; nothing to add; nothing to be. They literally consume their Power-to-Live. In the case of drug users, for instance, they even jeopardise their very physical existence.

4. We should not be reluctant to entertain ourselves because it is a source of pleasure and an intensifier of life – as long as we balance work and entertainment properly.

5. Parents who worry about their children who have a tendency to play too much are right. It is their role to give them a balanced way to live their lives.

6. The form of entertainment that we choose is, in most cases, in line with the main aspirations of our Power-to-Live. In that sense it does reinforce what we value and care about. It tells us something about the key parts of our Power-to-Live.

7. An excess of stimulation of some elements of our Power-to-Live (through work) can be balanced by the choice of complementary entertainment activities, e.g. a highly intellectual person will get into sport and physical activities.

5. Where do I go from here?

It is maybe time to stop again and examine your Way-to-Live in a more systematic fashion.

Our suggestion is to go to the third part of the book and start to work on your *personal journal*. This is how you could proceed:

Step 1. Look first at the various parts of the journal.

Step 2. Record in the journal (pick the parts that you feel more interesting and relevant for you) what happens to you. We suggest that you do it the following way:

- Describe the situation that you were (are) involved in

- Identify what you did (your own behaviour)

- Examine the impact of your behaviour on you and your life.

Step 3. Refrain from over-analysing what you did and what happened. Close the journal and let it rest for a while.

Step 4. Go back to what you wrote and get some key learning out of it.

Step 5. Try to find somebody that you trust who could play the sounding board role for you.

This is only one way to use the journal to enhance your PTL. Feel free to use it any way... Actually, the best way is the one that you will invent yourself!

What are the leadership implications?

Leaders are facing some major challenges in relation to the Way-to-Live:

1. Redefining work
2. Enhancing life
3. Avoiding boredom.

Redefining work

Yes, work is the process by which we activate our vital functions and accomplish our PTL.

Defined this way work is obviously essential to our existence. Leaders must therefore look at jobs and professional activities as an important part of people's lives and make every attempt to match their team members' work with their Power Maps. By leading others, they can to a large extent contribute to their personal achievements and happiness.

It is thus the responsibility of the leader to make sure that:

1. Team members achieve their work objectives (a condition for survival and maybe growth).

2. Team members have a chance to activate their PTLs through their jobs.

3. Team members help each other in the accomplishments of their deep aspirations.

Enhancing life

A job – according to the PTL model – is more than a job! The leader of the future will have to invest more time and talents in:

- Giving a fair chance to people to learn more about their deep aspirations through their jobs.

- Helping people find the right way (for themselves) to fulfil their aspirations while at work.

- Designing jobs together with their team members to make sure that the work objectives are achieved and the team members' desires met to the largest possible extent.

It is getting more and more obvious that the separation between private and professional lives is artificial at best and destructive at worst.

It is one's life as a whole that we are talking about!

The job part of the life is unquestionably a very important one. People spend a big chunk of their lives doing a job. And let's keep in mind that most of them go to work with their aspirations and come home bringing with them their frustrations!

That's what the PTL model emphasises. A leader is getting more and more involved not only in making sure that the team delivers great outputs but *also in enhancing people's lives though their jobs.*

AVOIDING BOREDOM

Remember that boredom is a signal that the PTL sends to itself to indicate that our vital functions are being kept idle and that we are therefore not responding to our very calling, which is to accomplish our PTL.

So the leader's role, here again, is to make sure that people are fully occupied in their Power-to-Live, so that they don't fall into boredom and always have the impression that they are responding to the needs of their PTL. This can only be achieved not only if people are kept busy but if their jobs closely correspond to their personal Power Maps.

CONCLUSION

If people are really what they do, then leaders must make sure that they have a fair opportunity to do something meaningful!

A sentimentalist is simply one who desires to have the luxury of an emotion without paying for it.

Oscar Wilde

7. ...and I am what I feel

What is it?

Emotions are a key element to our Way-to-Live. Emotions are the way by which we know if our PTL is in good shape or not.

They tell us where we stand with our Project-to-Live as well as what we need in order to be in better shape.

They also help us decide on the next direction to give to our PTL. They give some orientation to our actions.

So that we can say that emotions precede and generate actions, and that actions in turn lead to new emotions, in a kind of perpetual cycle.

Without emotions we are lost! It would be like driving a car in unknown territory with no dashboard and so signs on the road...

What's in it for me?

This chapter will guide you into the exploration of your emotions and the role they play in your life. It will explain why you feel what you feel and have the needs and desires that you have. It will also provide some tips on how to listen to your emotions and take them in good consideration.

You should know that there is a test on emotions in Part II of the book. We advise you to take the test *before reading this chapter*. It will be much more meaningful if you proceed that way.

Actually, we recommend you do the following:

- First, stop reading the chapter now and take the test without looking at the debriefing;

- Second, come back to the chapter and go through it very carefully;

- Third, when you are finished with this chapter, you go back to the test and read its debriefing section.

What is the red thread?

The four questions and the issue covered in this chapter are:

1. What are my emotions telling me, and why?
2. What are my emotions made of?
3. Why should I listen to my emotions?
4. How can we define happiness?

1. What are my emotions telling me, and why?

Our emotions are what we use to take stock of our PTL. They are the mode of our Way-to-Live by which we become aware of the state of accomplishment of our PTL as well of the changes required to ensure its perpetuation.

Let's remember that our actions are the behaviours that we use to alter the elements of the world in our favour.

Emotions are the measures that we use to evaluate the present and potential degree of accomplishment of our Project-to-Live.

Emotions are yardsticks or indicators.

Through our emotions we assess the state of progress of our PTL; through our actions we further implement our PTL. They are two distinct and complementary forms of our Way-to-Live.

To put it simply, we could say:

- I feel good (my PTL is in good shape, I am doing the right thing, my vital functions are activated the right way, I am expanding...)

- I feel bad (my PTL is in trouble, I am not using my Power-to-Live the right way...)

2. What are my emotions made of?

Emotions are made of two interconnected components, i.e. our *impressions* and our *desires*.

IMPRESSIONS

Our impressions are the signal we receive from our PTL telling us (itself) where we stand. Good impressions signify that we are doing OK, bad impressions are a warning that our PTL is in trouble and that we must do something about it.

Our impressions are of two kinds: *sensations* and *feelings*.

- *Sensations* refer to an immediate impression, something that we are actually experiencing in terms of pleasure or pain. Our sensations can be 'physical', as when we react to sensual delight or exquisite fragrances or repulsive taste, or 'mental', as when we feel sadness, joy or boredom.

    - Question: What kind of sensations do you have right now?

- *Feelings* refer to the impressions that we experience towards a person, an event or an object, in so far as they have the potential to affect our PTL. Our feelings are, so to speak, differed sensations. I like or dislike a person, an object or an event according to my estimate of whether it will impact my PTL favourably or unfavourably. Thus our feelings are always a variation of *love* or *hate*. Feelings play an extremely important role in the realisation of our PTL. It is through them that we attribute a positive or negative charge to the elements of the world (with regard to our PTL).

    - Question: Can you name three people who have had a powerful impact on your life, let us say, over the last five years? What are your feelings towards them?

We are able, as everyone has experienced, to perceive an enormous range of different feelings. However, as underlined below, it is interesting to understand that they can be classified in a series of negative–positive couples, of which they are all a form or variation.

1. Our feelings towards the *world in general*. They are all variations of worry or hope; we shift from worry to hope and vice versa according to whether we feel that the world is opposed to our PTL or feel, on the contrary, that the world is supportive of us.

Self-assessment exercise: What are your worries right now? What is your most important hope? How do you feel towards the world in general?

– My main worries are:

– My hope is:

– Towards the world and life in general, I feel...

2. Our feelings regarding *our own behaviour*. They are all variations of guilt and confidence. We feel *guilty* if we have the impression that we have been in some way remiss in carrying out our PTL and may therefore not be able to make it! We feel *confident* if we have the feeling that what we do (and are able to do) is constructive and in line with the requirements of our PTL ('we are doing the right things').

    Self-assessment exercise: What are you confident about now? Do you feel guilty about something?

    – I feel confident because...

    – I feel guilty because...

3. Our feelings about *others* and what's happening with them. They are all variations of empathy, a result of the fact that we tend to identify with the other's PTL. We feel *sorry* (pity) for someone who is unlucky and suffering and feel *close to and happy for* someone who is succeeding with his or PTL.

    These feelings, however, can be and generally are mitigated by the love/hate feelings we will have for these same people in so far as they are liable to impact our PTL.

    Self-assessment exercise: Any sorry feelings right at this minute? Do you feel quite close to someone at this instant?

    – I feel sorry for...

    – I am happy for...

    – But at the same time I am wary of or confident regarding so and so because ...

4. Our feelings about *others' judgement of us*. They are all forms of shame or pride; we feel *shame* if we feel that

they have no respect for us or for what we did, and *proud* if we feel that they admire or look up to us.

Self-assessment exercise: Are you proud? Do you feel ashamed?

– Yes, I am proud of...

– Yes, I feel ashamed because...

DESIRES

Desires follow our impressions (sensations and feelings) and are the form under which our Will-to-Live drives our Power-to-Live.

They are the stimuli that we need to move on with our PTL.

It works as follows: first, our impressions tell us where we stand regarding our PTL, and in turn our desires give a direction or a course of action to be taken. Our desires are then satisfied through our actions.

At every moment in time, we are subject to a multitude of conflicting desires that correspond to all the different impressions that inhabit us during that same time. That means:

1. That we must understand what those desires are and what they mean for our PTL

2. That we must choose and identify what we want to do (action)

3. That we must prioritise our actions and decide on what's best and most urgent

4. That we must agree to leave unsatisfied some of the desires which cannot be fulfilled right away

5. That we need to learn how to monitor the accomplishment of our desires so that we do not overdo what has to be done to satisfy the requirements of our PTL.

Desires can be regrouped into two main categories, i.e. the desires for change (for instance, to alter our Power-to-Live according to the impressions we have and to make it ever more favourable to our PTL) and the desire not to change (or desire for conservation), so that we maintain the status quo of our Power-to-Live perceived (through our impressions) as being advantageous to our PTL.

Questions
Are you experiencing any clear-cut desires right now? What are they? What are they telling you about your PTL? What are you going to do about them?

3. Why should I listen to my emotions?

If our emotions are the echoes of a never-ending dialogue between our Will-to-Live and our Power-to-Live, it is quite important for us to listen to what our emotions are conveying.

Part of our natural identity is to be emotional. We experience sensations, feelings and desires which are guiding us (if we listen properly) in the conduct of our lives.

So, again, emotions are a source of information of crucial importance for us. We must learn how to care about them and read them the right way so that we understand them correctly.

One of their most valuable aspects is that they tell us something about what is going on deep inside us, sometimes at a subconscious level that we are not accustomed to explore and analyse.

The process of listening to our emotions could be spelled out the following way:

Step 1. Acknowledge the very nature and intensity of the emotions that you are experiencing in a given situation (fear, sadness, anger...)

Step 2. Identify what the emotions are related to or what triggered them (a success, a failure, a comment, another person's reaction...)

Step 3. Analyse what the emotions are telling you about your Power-to-Live ('I am upset because I believe strongly in being responsible and my boss did not trust me') as well as about the overall status of your Will-to-Live ('I am depressed; this is not what I should be doing...')

Step 4. Draw a lesson out of the analysis and decide on what you should do next to improve your specific or overall situation. It could be, 'I shall talk to my boss to get a better understanding of what he wants, and explain to him my need for trust and autonomy.' Or, 'I shall start to explore other professional options to have a better alignment between what I want deep down inside and my professional activities.'

Step 5. Put things into perspective and reflect on what the entire process means for you.

We are 'emotional' beings, and that's great. To suppress the experience and the expression of emotions is a major mistake in anybody's life. Not only does it not make sense to fight against our emotions but it can actually be harmful to do so. We need to learn to decipher what our emotions are telling us and then act upon, not the emotions themselves, but on our Power-to-Live in its different components.

If we feel bad, we'll try to contain or get rid of the cause of the negative feeling; if we feel good, we'll do our very best to preserve and extend the cause of our pleasure.

Emotions are the instruments that we desperately need to manage our Power-to-Live and therefore our PTL.

A final word about 'overreacting' emotionally to people and situations. What does it mean?

Emotional overreactions could mean that we have behaved on a very short-term basis and forgotten about the longer-term effects of the actions we have taken on the spur of the moment. In short, we have been short-sighted and have ignored the more fundamental needs of our PTL. Later, we regret it.

By overreacting, we go for what seems imperative and urgent and eventually overlook some of the more fundamental needs of our PTL. The lesson here is that we must develop our ability to put things into perspective and grow from some difficult experience. That being said, we must acknowledge that *some* strong short-term reactions to emotions are valid because they are the safeguards for our PTL. This is sometimes the case when we are scared and angry. Such an emotion can usefully lead to an immediate mobilisation of our means of reaction and enable us to cope with a threat and survive. But even then, we may still overreact and even panic!

Overreacting could also mean that something (or someone) has touched a sensitive or highly valued spot in our Power-to-

Live. Our reaction is telling us something about the importance of the various components of our Power Map. Some are more important than others.

We must also realise that to learn not to be 'emotional' as a principle is pure nonsense. Not to be emotional would mean to suppress and ignore some vital signals from our deeper self (PTL) and therefore miss an opportunity to know more and better about us and grow.

4. How can we define happiness?

Hold it for a minute here! Can you come up with your own definition of happiness before reading on?

- For me, happiness is...

Let us now compare notes.

What does happiness mean? According to our definition, happiness is a positive impression, a sensation or a feeling of well-being which tells us something about the state of our PTL: we are in good shape. We are on the right track. We are doing the right thing.

Another way to look at it is to say, 'I am happy because it seems that my Power-to-Live is quite capable of satisfying my Will-to Live.'

The term happiness, however, has a strong connotation implying a notion of permanence as regards the state it defines. That can be dangerous because, as we all know, life by definition and experience is anything but stable.

So what does it mean then?

In addition to what we said above, the use of the term happiness can only mean one of two things: either it is just a figure of speech or it can also show a refusal or lack of awareness.

In the first case, probably the most frequent, one will speak of happiness to indicate that the positive impressions one feels at a given moment supersede by far the negative ones – negative impressions that for the moment we can decide to ignore.

This means that when we claim to be happy, we do not really imply that everything is well in the best of all possible worlds, but rather that we are paying more attention to what's going well (still according to our PTL requirements) or simply pushing aside our feeling of worry. Or to put it differently, that we give a predominant place to our feeling of hope.

The first way is called balancing our lives; the second one is more of a lucid delusion by which, again, we choose to voluntarily focus on the positive side of things and consciously forget those aspects that can affect us unfavourably.

As for the second scenario, where we claim to be happy (even in a permanent way), it denotes in our eyes a lack of lucidity or of courage. Let's quote the French poet Mallarmé who wrote: 'He who says "I am happy" is really saying "I am a fool" or "I am a coward".'

What Mallarmé meant by that is that whatever positive things could happen to us in our existence, our Power-to-Live always remains subject to negative influences that can threaten our PTL.

So what we are suggesting here is enjoy happiness when you experience a good match between your Power-to-Live and the life situations that you are in. It does happen from time to time – fortunately! It is natural. It is good. However, keep in mind that those states cannot (will not) last for ever. They are temporary states of mind which will be necessarily followed by struggles and... pain. That's what living is all about!

What are the leadership implications?

YOU AND YOUR EMOTIONS

Before presenting a few leadership guidelines on emotions, we suggest that you assess yourself on a scale from one to ten (1 = 'I am not good at this'; 10 ='I am very good at this').

How good are you at:

1. Paying attention to your own emotions

2. Reading your boss's mood

3. Expressing your emotions in a constructive way

4. Allowing people to ventilate their emotions

5. Looking at emotions in a positive way

6. Getting other people's emotions in the open

7. Turning negative emotions into something useful

8. Creating a good emotional environment within your team

9. Understanding the message in emotions

10. Taking action following people's expressions of emotions?

DEBRIEFING

- If your total score is between 1 and 30: It seems that you do not care much about emotions. Do you even know that they exist? Watch out, that could play tricks on you...

- If your score is between 30 and 70: Good for you! You know that emotions are an important part of human life. You are sensitive (smart) enough to identify them, read through them and use them.

- If your score is between 70 and 100: This is a bit excessive! You are maybe focusing too much on the emotional dimension of work, forgetting perhaps that there are still some objectives to achieve.

THE POWER OF HAPPINESS

One of the big questions that has been troubling leaders for quite some time is: Do happy people perform better than unhappy people?

Yes, we do know now for sure that satisfied and happy people perform much better than unhappy ones. Why?

Because by being happy, people just show that they are doing things that are in line with what they want to do. In other words that their job requirements are in line with their aspirations.

It is very simple: Give people what they are dying to do and the sky is the limit!

As a leader can you now measure the degree of happiness of your team members according to the following characteristics?

In your team, do people:

1. Laugh a lot

2. Share their joy with others

3. Celebrate each other's successes

4. Relax together
5. Listen to some music while working
6. Show excitement (at least from time to time)
7. Help each other
8. Care about others' lives
9. Encourage each other
10. Say that their jobs are exciting?

If you answer negatively at least three times, there is a good chance that you have a morale problem in your team. Be careful!

Too many yeses could also mean that the team is on a free ride. Again, be careful!

Another way of looking at this issue is to reflect on the leadership's ability to create positive emotions.

POSITIVE EMOTIONS

Positive emotions are mainly defined as emotions loaded with:

- Good feelings about oneself (I like the way I am)
- Optimism regarding tomorrow (the power of hope)
- Open attitude towards others (they are good for me)

As a leader, where do you stand regarding these three traits?

The noble type of man feels himself *to be the determiner of values, he does not need to be approved of, he judges: 'What harms me is harmful in itself...'*

Friedrich Nietzsche

8. What is right? What is wrong?

What is it?

This is about organising and managing our lives so that we function meaningfully and effectively. It concerns the economy of life, or how we choose our courses of action. It is also about deciding what's right and wrong for us.

This follows the presentation of the three main parts of the Project-to-Live:

1. **The Will-to-Live** or the drive that we share with all living beings towards the perpetuation of our lives.

2. **The Power-to-Live** or the means by which we (in our own and unique way) make use of the world (which is us!) to implement our PTL.

3. **The Way-to-Live** or everything that we feel and do (our emotions and our actions).

It is now time to have a good look at how it all ties together to form our day-to-day existence. We call this the *art of living*.

What's in it for me?

This is presumably the most practical part of the book. It will give you an opportunity to see how the PTL works in practice for you. It will attempt to draw the pieces together and help you to decide on what's suitable for you!

You can also expect to get some ideas on the way you balance your life in general, manage your personal and work lives, and finally check on your own art of living.

The meaning of *ethics* will also be reviewed and explained in line with the PTL model, so that you can reflect on why and how you tend to resort to a code of behaviour when carrying out your existence.

It could be very useful for you to go through the test on 'The art of living' (see Part III of the book) at the same time that you are reading this chapter. It's up to you...

What is the red thread?

The chapter will focus on five interrogations and the usual issue, i.e.:

1. Am I free to do what I want?
2. How do I know that I am succeeding (or failing)?
3. Can I balance work, entertainment and rest more effectively?
4. What is my code of conduct? Do I have one?
5. How can I improve my personal art of living?

1. Am I free to do what I want?

This is a question that we all ask at one time or another in our life. How free am I? Can I just decide what I should want and what I should do? Or am I, at least to some extent, determined by some forces that are beyond my own will?

The answer according to us is... *no*. In fact, we are not that free at all!

There is no question that during the implementation of our lives our behaviour is bound by several constraints that are inherent in the very nature and structure of our PTL. We cannot be free. Freedom is a virtual impossibility. Sorry.

Whaaa...! Do you agree with the above statements?

We call these 'the constraints of life'. We have no choice but to go by their rules.

We are indeed subject to three main constraints that determine our behaviour:

1. Our Will-to-Live: our principle desire, objective, motivation is given to us right from the beginning! Whatever decision we take will always be governed by this overwhelming constraint which is 'I want (I need) to perpetuate my existence'.

2. Our Power-to-Live: Whenever we decide to act, we do it in accordance with the means that are available to us to

do so at that very point in time: our intelligence, our knowledge, our skills, the 'external' circumstances, and so on. This is therefore another series of constraints that determine our behaviour and limit our freedom.

3. The economic equation of life.

This economic equation takes into account three factors, which we have already discussed earlier but which we now need to see as tightly tied together. Indeed, any activity that we undertake will be evaluated according to the three following factors:

- Factor 1: Its output
- Factor 2: The mobilisation of our vital functions as we engage in it
- Factor 3: Its cost.

THE OUTPUT

The idea here is that any action or behaviour must be conducive to the preservation and, even better, to the enhancement of our Power-to-Live.

The more our behaviour tends to conserve and strengthen our Power-to-Live, the more we will perceive it as valuable. We rarely do anything without having at least some idea of what we expect in return. It is their *expected output* that in many cases drives our actions. We do what we think will make us more able to accomplish our PTL.

It is thus in our interest to select the behaviours from which we can expect an optimum return for our PTL. At least, that's what the first part of the theory says. In practice, some other factors are going to interfere and even possibly dictate some less efficient behaviour.

Questions

Select some of your recent actions (at work or at home) and analyse why you did them. In other words, identify the expected outputs which determined your decision to act.

THE MOBILISATION OF OUR VITAL FUNCTIONS

As we have seen before, we have an urge to ensure the greatest possible mobilisation of our Power-to-Live.

We must make sure that our vital functions (brain, mind, body...) are kept busy. We do this almost unconsciously, automatically.

The non-utilisation of our Power-to-Live leads, as we know now, to boredom. We must avoid it and get involved in something (either work or entertainment).

What we are saying here is that the need to do something and be busy is intrinsically compulsory.

We feel alive when we use our means to live in order to realise our PTL. And the more we mobilise our faculties, the more alive we feel, and in consequence we feel happier too.

Questions

Do you remember a time when you were deeply and actively involved in some activity? How was it? What about another time when you had nothing to do?

THE COST

The third factor is the cost involved in any of our activities.

Every activity that we undertake requires a certain expense, and thus leads to a certain degree of weakening of our capacity to ensure our survival.

How can this be?

It is true for the two following reasons (think about it!):

1. Action has a cost. Whatever we do will cost us in terms of our Power-to-Live. We will at the very least spend energy and time, two important ingredients of our Power-to-Live.

    Question: Think about yesterday and everything you did. Can you identify the cost of your actions?

2. A decision that I take to act in a certain direction implies that I renounce going another way and achieving something different. As the saying goes, 'To choose is to renounce.'

    Question: How many times in the last five years did you have to choose a course of action at the expense of something else?

The conclusion here is that the cost factor implies that we must make sure that the action we are contemplating is worth our time and effort or, in other terms, that when we combine both the expected return on our effort and the rate of involvement of our vital functions that this action implies, they will come out higher than the cost we are putting in terms of our Power-to-Live.

Thus the three factors pulled together can lead to what we describe as being *the economic equation of our activity.*

It goes as follows:

Value of an activity = Expected useful output + Rate of mobilisation − Cost or: $V = O + M - C$

If the value analysis (before acting) speaks in favour of a specific action, then we should go for it!

If not, we should refrain from acting and think about other more favourable alternatives.

It is clear that we are all constantly subject to tensions and conflicts coming from the coexistence of these three vital ingredients of life. Here are a couple of examples:

- The cost of doing something is sometimes so high that it is not worth undertaking it. It weighs too heavily against the expected result and rate of mobilisation: I can decide to go on vacation, but then my work is not going to be finished on time and I will be in trouble.

- What's most useful for me is not necessarily what mobilises me the most intensely and vice versa: I can decide to go for a promotion, which will prevent me writing the book that I have been dying to write and which would have stimulated me greatly; or this activity that I am contemplating is very useful and will increase my Power-to-Live, but by God, it is so boring that I don't think I can get into it!

It seems that we generally go for the options that offer the best compromise for our PTL. Life appears to be a succession of choices or self-regulations of our Power-to-Live. Mistakes in our choices and their implementation can happen, of course, and be the source of pain, bad feelings and sickness. But that's only because our Power-to-Live is far from perfect and also because external circumstances don't always work in our favour.

It is true that we may not always act in accordance with our best interests. However, we usually act to the best of our judgement and means! If we find out, after the fact, that we should and could have behaved otherwise, then that should serve as a lesson for the next time, and make us learn/grow/expand.

The silliest thing of course is to feel guilt or regret, since we are what we are, and have behaved as we have just because of that! If we had indeed acted differently, then we would not be who we are! However, we cannot avoid feeling guilt or regret, because these impressions reflect the judgement we make after the fact of our aptitude to accomplish our PTL. Even if we know that we couldn't have acted otherwise, we still would have preferred to have been able to do so.

Let's imagine that after having seriously thought over the issue I made a decision that didn't turn out to be the right one. Should I feel guilty? Certainly not, because being who I am I just couldn't have decided differently. Therefore, whatever bad feeling I might have about my mistake is merely an evaluation of myself and my capacity to carry out my PTL! If I feel bad, what I am telling myself is that I wish I were someone else, which in reality is absurd! Therefore, it's better to replace guilt, fear and regrets with a capacity to learn from my mistakes, so that by doing so I enhance my Power-to-Live and lessen the chances of doing the wrong thing a second time.

2. How do I know that I am succeeding (or failing)?

Or, 'What are the criteria that I can use to measure the success of my PTL?' To put it simply, the question is, how do we know that our PTL is in good shape and working?

Let's examine two other questions before answering that one:

Question 1: Is the purpose of our lives merely to preserve ourselves, i.e. to ensure our basic survival, or is it to expand and strengthen our Power-to-Live?

The answer to the first question is that it is a misleading debate! The PTL as a project of self-perpetuation implies both the conservation and the increase of its Power-to-Live. The latter is the condition of the former. If my purpose in life is to accomplish my Will-to-Live, then my aim can only be to constantly strengthen my Power-to-Live. It is by growing that we guarantee the success of our PTL. If we don't grow we shrink, because the world will be changing anyway, and in a way that is not to our advantage!

Question 2: Why should we try to measure the accomplishment of our PTL?

We must learn how to assess (this answers the second question) the accomplishment of our PTL to avoid some major pitfalls, such as being on the wrong track, not capitalising properly on our Power-to-Live, losing a sense of direction, wasting our time and energy, feeling depressed, having a sense of being lost...

So, yes, it is of great value to stop from time to time and assess where we stand with our lives (or PTL).
How do we do that?
In fact there are two basic indicators of the accomplishment of our PTL:

- duration
- intensity.

Duration or time is unquestionably the primary measure that we can use. Like any other project, the PTL is inscribed in time, aimed at the future. No time, no project, therefore no PTL – and no more life for us!
Duration is nothing else than the continuation of our PTL as long as possible. My Will-to-Live cannot be satisfied if I am not around to take care of it! My PTL can only be as long as it lasts. It is that simple.
So we'll do almost everything to remain alive (with some paradoxes, such as suicide and personal sacrifices, which we'll examine at the end of the book).

Intensity or the degree of mobilisation of our Power-to-Live is the other way to measure the accomplishment of our PTL. Since our vocation is to live, to accomplish our PTL, the more we have the impression that this is happening, the more we feel in conformity with our very purpose, and therefore the better we feel!

In some cases, we are ready to sacrifice the length of our PTL for the sake of its intensity. We sometimes decide to go for something very short-term in our life knowing very well that it will cost us in the future (if we get there). We all have seen people renouncing an uncertain future in favour of a present more tangible satisfaction (here and now). Examples are plentiful: smoking, drinking, using drugs and practising violent and dangerous sports...

What we want is *to live*. We want to live with 'passion'. We want to feel the essence of our self being activated, worked out, used and... fulfilled.

We must recognise that in many life situations there is a trade-off between duration and intensity. We can surely often decide to live dangerously at the expense of safety!

It is also true that we can renounce some immediate satisfactions for the sake of tomorrow. We invest for the future. We care about the expected output of our actions so as to preserve the possibility of a tomorrow. Parents are very good at drawing their children's attention to this aspect of life.

3. Can I balance work and entertainment and rest more effectively?

This issue is widely debated in today's world (at least in the West). The obvious answer is *yes*. The real question is, how do I do it?

First, let's point out that each individual is made of his own Power-to-Live, different from any other person's. Each man or woman experiences circumstances that are particular to him or her. We all construct our reality according to our PTL.

It means that the way we direct our lives, decide on a course of action and interpret all the situations that we experience as human beings is a matter of personal evaluation.

Study the following propositions carefully:

- Only you can tell for sure if the activity you have undertaken has a fundamental purpose or not.

- Only you can decide if an action is work (contributing to your PTL) or entertainment (creating a sense of occupation and an illusion of being useful).

- Only you can decide if you prefer to live securely with the perspective of a longer duration of your existence or whether you want to live intensely at the risk of reducing your lifetime.

- Only you can judge and master the way to achieve your PTL within the circumstances that you face. Others can advise you on what to decide, do and accomplish. However nobody can decide for you what's right or wrong. This is our ultimate choice according to the needs of your specific PTL.

The way each of us responds to the demands of the Will-to-Live is our personal decision. It is our own business.

Experience has shown that there is an infinity of ways of fulfilling one's PTL.

The only acceptable position we can have towards others is to judge their behaviour in relation to how they favour (or hamper) our own PTL, or others'. As we said earlier, we will love or hate other people according to how they impact on our existence or that of people that we identify with, including themselves. But to pass any other kind of judgement is abusive, since at the end of the day they are certainly responsible for their own PTL.

So now back to the question of balancing our Way-to-Live more effectively: How can we do it?

The answer is quite simple (at least on paper!):

- Phase 1. By having a better and deeper understanding of the various ingredients of our PTL.

- Phase 2. By writing down the economic equation of our behaviour and analysing its various components as they apply to us.

- Phase 3. By deciding on a course of action and listening to our emotions during its implementation, so that we know at any moment where we stand and what kind of corrective actions we should take (if any).

4. What is my code of conduct? Do I have one?

Of course, you have one... Everybody has a code of conduct. Life would not be possible without one.

We call that code, 'ethics', and by ethics we mean a code of rules to which we submit our day-to-day behaviour in order to accomplish our PTL.

Let's probe the most common questions about ethics:

1. What are ethics?

2. Why do I need ethics?

3. What are the key differences (if any) between ethics and morals?

4. Can I be immoral?

5. Where does that leave me?

1. WHAT ARE ETHICS?

Ethics are a set of ready-made answers that we refer to and use in our daily life. They form a short cut. They are a set of guidelines that we resort to when we are in a situation of tension, in a dilemma, in a conflict of interest, or where we have a choice between one or several way of behaving in order to achieve our PTL.

The conflict can be purely internal or between individuals.

Internal: the conflict will be generally between an immediate advantage that a course of behaviour can offer and a more remote reward which that behaviour seems to present. We experience a dilemma. We struggle. We are not sure what to do.

Ethics will help us solve the problem by suggesting a solution. For instance, I can have a choice between playing some game or just basking in the sun so as to experience pleasant sensations (entertainment), or instead going to work on a difficult and yet worthwhile project (work).

Such a conflict is typical of an ethical dilemma. To resolve it (fast and easily), most people will resort to a private ethical code that they use almost automatically (without thinking), so that they have the proper balance between entertainment and work, and this for the best interest of the PTL.

Between individuals: In the same way, when my own personal interest is in conflict with that of another person, the use of my code of ethics will help me to deal with this situation.

Instead of just going for my immediate and very short-term (in some cases) interest (just for the sake of my own PTL at the expense of the other person's), I shall compromise and go for a longer-term output. For example, my selfish (PTL) interest is telling me that I should go through the door first, whereas my code of ethics is telling me that I should be polite and wait my turn. This ethical (because it's coded) behaviour may put some strain on me, but there is no question that the overall benefit will be greater that the cost.

To summarise, ethics is a code of conduct whose purpose is to determine a particular course of action when a conflict of interest (internal or external) is raised within our PTL. Ethics will help us find a quick solution so that we do not have to go through the identification and evaluation of the best way to handle it. In short, our PTL is taking advantage of that standardised way of deciding and acting.

2. WHY DO WE NEED ETHICS?

We need ethics for the following reasons:

- It makes our behaviour more economical
- It helps us to be more stable
- It leads to more and greater efficiency.

More economical

We are confronted during our lives with situations that repeat themselves more or less regularly and identically. They challenge our PTL in the same fashion. They are standard situations or events. For instance:

- We can be tempted by some objects that do not belong to us
- We are inclined not to tell the truth
- We are nagged by a desire that we know we should not give in to because if we do we'll regret it later.

In those common situations, we can behave in two different ways:

The first is to ask ourselves each time again what is the best attitude to adopt by weighing the pros and cons of the options available in our minds. Such a calculation will inevitably cost us a certain amount of time and energy – time and energy which could be used for a better purpose for the sake of our PTL.

The second is to make a quick reference to our code of ethics and solve the problem diligently and painlessly. By fixing in advance the way we should behave when confronted with such standard situations, we save time and effort. We save ourselves for something more important. The economic advantage for our PTL is enormous.

For instance: I get up in the morning and one of the first things I do is shower and, if I am a man, shave. Should I do it this very morning? What would be the advantages and disadvantages of showering and shaving today? Or of *not* going through those usual (and often boring) motions? Rather than asking myself every day those tedious questions, I will just apply what my code of ethics tells me: 'Every morning, unless there is a good and special reason not to do it, you will shower and shave.' Period. By doing that, I save time, energy and a lot of hassle.

More stable

By establishing in advance that we will behave in a predictable and generally accepted way when confronted by standard situations, we make our lives easier and more consistent. It is indeed in our interest to do so.

Easier, because we decide on our actions without even thinking.

It facilitates our relationships with other people. We know what to expect from them and they know what to expect from us.

More consistent, because people's behaviours are basically in line with a common set of rules and standards. The benchmark is the same.

Everybody benefits from the common code of ethics. It makes our social life much more coherent and manageable. We can expect what will happen next and what the consequences of our actions will be.

More effective

Each time we apply an ethical rule of conduct, it becomes a test or a proof of its validity. Ethical rules benefit from the learning accumulated in the course of our personal and collective experience.

Ethics become part of our culture. Being continuously challenged and adjusted, they are more or less accepted by all as the best way to act in a given standard situation.

The people who do not believe in them, or think that there are better ways of coping with the requirements of the standard situation that we experience every day, challenge them.

Ethics get adjusted to the new demands of the time. Things change around. New technologies are invented and used, nature evolves, and new generations of men and women take over. The relative character of our ethics, their contingency and their cultural variations explain why the principles that compose them can never be considered as untouchable, absolute and immutable. The only exception is 'Thou shalt live!', because that is the very essence of our being.

Our ethics proceed from our personal and collective history. Both are, by definition, in constant evolution. We change, and the situations that we experience never stay the same either. 'Standard situation' does not mean perfectly identical situation.

It is clear that any attempt to freeze our ethical code into a pattern which corresponds to a given moment in time is only a sign of an effort to stop our evolution and can only lead to tension, utopianism and ineffectiveness.

Our PTL demands that we take the changes occurring in our environment into account and examine our code of ethics with a critical (vigilant) eye.

Ethics are a product of our experience of life and also the means by which we perfect our behaviour.

3. WHAT ARE THE KEY DIFFERENCES (IF ANY) BETWEEN ETHICS AND MORALS?

Let's state once more that ethics as a code of conduct form an integral part of our PTL. Without ethics we cannot succeed with our Project-to-Live.

A lack of ethics would make our lives much more difficult (if not impossible) and jeopardise our PTL.

The term 'ethics', as we have defined it, covers the totality of our behaviour. But there is a particular sector of our behaviour that is very important, because we are 'social animals'; namely, our behaviour as it pertains to other people. The part of our ethics that codifies our behaviour towards other people is something we have given a special name to, just to single it out because of the important role it plays in our lives: we call it morals.

The first question that comes to mind, however, when we think of our conduct towards others is: 'Why do we care at all?' Because, when you come to think of it, if our PTL is all there is for us, why should we be concerned about what happens to other people, and why on earth should we go out of our way to help them? In other words, what can be the foundation of our moral behaviour?

It is well known that traditions all over the world and throughout time have often resorted to a transcendent reference to explain why we should care about each other. The Christian religion, for example, sees in charity (based on compassion and love) one of the highest virtues that believers must practise to ensure their salvation ('We love because God first loved us').

Our contention is different. We strongly believe that our concern and care about others result (like anything else that we do or feel) from our will to accomplish our personal PTL. It serves us to behave that way!

Two types of situations can be mentioned in which we care for others:

1. It is clear that in many personal and professional situations, we pay attention to other people's needs (i.e. their PTL) because it is in our obvious interest to do so, like when we:

- Care about our children, because we see them as an extension of our own PTL.

- Help our boss, because we expect some reward in return.

- Give to charity, because we expect to be paid back in the next world or get social recognition.

Question: Can you find some personal examples of this kind of commitment to others for our own sake?

2. The second example is more intriguing because it is characterised by the fact that our behaviour does not appear, at least not in an obvious way, to serve our own PTL.

The issue is, how can we reconcile the apparent contradiction between the self-centred demands of our Project-to-Live and the authentically unselfish behaviour that we show from time to time in our life? For instance, when we try to save somebody's life at the very serious risk of our own. How is it? Does this invalidate our contention that our PTL is in all cases the exclusive foundation of our behaviour in all its forms?

We do not think so. We contend that the two seemingly different foundations are actually both valid and identical. We claim that the foundation that justifies my intention to care for my fellow being in an unselfish manner is also part of my PTL. How come?

What explains it all, we believe, is our natural tendency to *identify* with others. It is the identification with other people, our fellow human beings, which leads us to care about them as if they were us, and therefore to favour their PTL as if they were our own.

It is this identification that is the foundation of my unselfish 'moral' conduct. It is none other than my PTL, or more precisely my personal PTL projected onto the other person. By identifying with the other person, I transfer in him (her) my personal PTL, and I hence behave as if I were dealing with myself.

A few illustrations will help understand what this identification process is all about:

- We admire somebody so much that we do many things to serve him or her, being strongly convinced that we, by the same token, serve ourselves ('I want to be like him/her').

- We 'pity' someone who is in a very distressing situation, feeling his or her pain as if it were our own ('It is happening to me').

- We grieve at somebody's death, when we are actually thinking about our own mortality.

- We are so much in love with somebody (or love our child, or our friend or parent) that our behaviour is totally geared towards pleasing him or her because that's what makes us happy (as if we were pleasing ourselves) – ('If I give her pleasure I have the feeling that I am reinforcing my own existence as I enhance hers').

So it seems that we are capable of unselfish acts towards others but that the bottom line is that our actions are still very selfish since it is our own PTL projected in others that underlies our behaviours.

Our conclusion is that since we have a tendency through our imagination to identify other people's PTL with our own, we will behave towards the others as if we were dealing with ourselves. And there should be nothing wrong with that, since it provides an explanation for our most altruistic and noble actions, which remains consistent with the all encompassing model of the PTL.

4. CAN I BE IMMORAL?

Immorality is the transgression of ethics. We are immoral when we overlook the principles that we have established to guide our behaviour. It happens when we opt for an action that we know is against our code of ethics.

Why in the world should we do that? Why should we act in a way that is not consistent with the rules that, in principle, are in favour of our PTL? Is it a sign of fatal sickness or anachronism?

The answer is very simple (and in line with the PTL model):

By acting in an immoral way, we still believe that we are serving our PTL and, even more, that we are doing it because our PTL requires it.

Situations of this kind generally reflect an opposition between an immediate temptation that responds to a pressing and short-term need of our PTL and the deeper desire to conform to the ethical code that we know suits our PTL in the longer term.

Here are a few simple illustrations:

- I know that lying goes against my code of conduct and yet in a given situation I'll feel a strong urge to lie to serve my immediate interest and avoid getting into trouble.

- I am aware that cheating on my spouse is wrong and yet I'll do it to satisfy a very short-term and strong desire.

- I am convinced that saying bad things about people is wrong. I still do it to enhance my own position in a particular situation.

It is clear that when the act is over and we have satisfied the more pressing desire that ethics forbade us, we will (in many cases, and assuming that we still believe that our code of ethics is right) recognise the immoral aspect of the conduct. We will even regret it in some cases. We can feel guilty and persuade ourselves not to do it again!

But if we come to realise that we keep breaching our code of ethics consistently, then it's probably time to revise the code itself, which may not be adapted any more to the interests of our PTL.

5. WHERE DOES THAT LEAVE ME?

It leaves you with the (hopefully) full realisation of the existence and importance of the so-called 'code of ethics' and its moral dimension.

We all tend to adopt and keep handy a set of rules of conduct that we can call upon when we experience some decision-making dilemma.

Again, let us restate the fact that ethics form a set of ready-made solutions that we use to confront the many situations which require decisions on our part, and to do it in such a way that we know will best serve our PTL.

We have created some of the rules through our experience and reflection. The others have been taught to us.

The questions we should ask ourselves are the following: How broad is the span of our code of ethics? Does it cover a large enough range of possible standard situations to effectively facilitate our existence, or are we often faced with circumstances before which we are powerless (we do not have an answer and we must ponder at length before deciding), or with only inadequate answers? Is it flexible enough and open to change?

In other words, is our behaviour to a sufficient extent predictable and constant enough, or is it more often left to our 'spur of the moment' best judgement and improvisation?

One reason why we might be suffering from a limited range

of ethics may well be that we fail to learn from our experiences.

We suggest that to learn how to manage our ethics is a key success factor in our lives. We must become wiser. And to be wise is to be knowledgeable of the world we are living in and to be familiar with the circumstances that impact on our existence so that we can decide on a stable reference of meaning as well as on a coherent code of ethics.

We hope that the PTL will serve the purpose of fulfilling the need of the reference and that you, the reader, will develop your ability to learn from each key decision you make.

That being said, let's remember as mentioned above that there can be moments and situations where our code of ethics is no longer efficient or valid. When we realise that we keep infringing a set of rules to satisfy our PTL we must question whether the rules have not become obsolete. It is our responsibility to make sure that our ethics are indeed serving our PTL and not the opposite! When our ethical code becomes out of date, which is bound to happen after some time, then we'd better revise it lest it becomes a burden rather than a useful tool!

What are the leadership implications?

LEADERSHIP TIP 1: GO WITH WHAT YOU HAVE

Isn't it true that very effective leaders focus on the individuals' strengths and build on what people can do or want to do? It is much more efficient to spend time and energy helping people improve on their natural and learned capacities instead of wasting them on the suppression of weaknesses.

LEADERSHIP TIP 2: GO WITH THE FLOW

Great leaders have a flair for what's in the air. They know what the flow is and in which direction the wind is blowing. They are sensitive enough to avoid going against the trend and adjust themselves to what's happening. They seize opportunities as they come. They spot good options inside as well as outside their organisations. They are not free but they thrive!

LEADERSHIP AND THE EQUATION OF LIFE

Let's review the equation of life: The value of an activity is the function of the expected useful output plus the rate of mobilisation minus the cost involved, i.e. $V = O + M - C$.

One leadership implication of the equation is that people will invest themselves in some action as long as:

- They perceive a *meaningful output* from what they are expected to do ('What's in it for me?').

- They see the required action as a source of *excitement and pleasure* ('Do I like it or not?').

- The cost involved is not too high ('How *painful* is it going to be?').

- So the art of leadership is in a way the ability to present actions to be implemented in such a way that people clearly see the benefits for them, the pleasure they will get out of their behaviours and the little cost involved.

THE ART OF LIVING

Leaders must distinguish between the people who are more interested in duration and those who are looking for intensity.

Duration

It is true that some people are more attracted to long-term activities which require patience and depth. These people are by and large reliable and the solid performers of the team. The leader should 'use' them as the backbone of the organisation.

Intensity

Some other people are more looking for the excitement of the moment. They sparkle with ideas and invest themselves completely and totally in short-term actions. They are the creative people of the organisation. As such they deliver outstanding outputs, but can be unreliable (you never know where you're going to be next).

CODE OF CONDUCT AND ETHICS

This is today one of the most critical dimensions of leadership. It is about the team and the company code of conduct. We believe that leaders should address (and review constantly) the following questions (please assess your company on a scale of 1 to 10. 1 is not at all; 10 is absolutely true):

I.8. What is right? What is wrong?

In our company, we:

- Have a clear idea of what's proper and not proper
- Know what the sanctions are if we transgress the company code of conduct
- Understand the rationale behind the code of conduct
- Know what ethics are about
- Discuss ethical issues openly and regularly
- Support fully and completely our ethical code
- Have a strong sense of social responsibility
- Walk the talk when dealing with ethical issues
- Have our corporate values in line with the legal requirements of the country in which we operate
- Behave according to a strong sense of social responsibility.

Over himself; over his own body and mind,
the individual is sovereign.

John Stuart Mill

9. Who is in charge?

What is it?

If the PTL (and its Will-to-Live) is the driver of our lives, then who is in charge? Who is responsible for my life? Or, who is in charge of what I am and what I am becoming?

Questions

It may be useful for you to devote a few minutes to answer some questions before reading our own answers (provocative as usual). So get your pencil!

- Do you feel in charge of your own life? Do not ponder too much. Just answer.

- What is your position regarding the existence of free will?

- How do you react to the following statement made by a young lady to her lover: 'My purpose in life is to serve Christ and enjoy swimming'?

- Can we be responsible without being free?

- Is it still possible to enjoy our life if there is no free will?

Keep your notes handy and move along now.

As human beings, we have always been concerned about the issue of *freedom or free will*. How free are we to determine our thoughts and behaviour? How much responsibility do we have for the actions that we take?

So this chapter is about freedom and responsibility. We are going to see how the PTL model can also help us with those two fundamental questions.

As we know, accomplishing our PTL is the absolute and exclusive duty we have, despite the fact that we do not have any responsibility for having been catapulted into the world of living beings. This gives to our lives a paradoxical dimension, with a tragic side, as we will see later in this chapter.

We own our lives without having the responsibility for what we are!

What's in it for me?

This is perhaps the most interesting and challenging part of the book. It will give you some tips on the following concerns that you must have (one way or another):

- Am I free?
- If not, what are the limits of my free will, or how predetermined is my behaviour?
- How can I be responsible if I am not free?
- Can I still choose?
- What do I need in order to face the 'imposed' challenges of my life?
- Is courage the answer to the tragic dimension of my life?
- If I am not free, why bother?

What is the red thread?

Here are the main questions and issues of this chapter:

- Can I act freely?
- Am I responsible?
- How can I cope with the tragic side of my existence?
- Is courage the answer?
- Is suicide an option?

1. Can I act freely?

This is about our liberty to act. It is about our *dignity* as human beings as well as about the responsibility that we have while living our lives.

The questions are:

- How free are we in deciding on our actions?

- How free are we to do what we have decided?
- Does the question about freedom make sense?

It is well known that these questions have been asked, probed and discussed in Western philosophy since the beginning of time. There has been no serious religion or philosophy ever since man started to communicate his thoughts that did not address those issues.

As human beings, we are all concerned one way or another about the extent of freedom that we enjoy, so that we can determine our behaviour and our identity. We want to know if we can do and be what we want. Don't you?

For us (in this book and according to the model) the key concern is, 'Does the PTL give an answer to the questions of freedom and responsibility?'

We have already said a few words about this subject in a previous chapter, but now it's time to go deeper into the matter.

We contend that the PTL model with its main component, i.e. the Will-to-Live, does indeed give us a straight (and for many people disturbing) answer.

What is it?

Let's look first at two premises before tackling this important and difficult question:

PREMISE 1

Let's state again in an unequivocal way that to live, to accomplish our PTL, is the absolute and exclusive obligation that we have. Not because we chose it, but precisely because it comes with our very existence as a PTL. There is nothing else. It is my purpose. It is a given. I am the reference. You are your reference. The freedom question should be asked within this framework.

Question

What is your gut feeling reaction to the above statement?

PREMISE 2

If there is to be a space for freedom (for us human beings), it can only lie downstream of the advent of the Project-to-Live. From the moment I am, I am as a Project-to-Live, and I do not have the option of choosing any other end than that. *I exist as a totally determined being as regards my most basic intent or purpose, which is my Will-to-Live.* If I may still enjoy any sort of freedom, it can only be at the levels of my Power-to-Live and Way-to-Live, in other words as regards the means and ways by which I will attempt to satisfy my will to live.

Question

Does the above affirmation satisfy you? If not, why not?

Let's backtrack a bit and go deeper into the exploration of this very exciting (and fundamental) interrogation.

Let's look at the meaning of freedom.

Our first impression of freedom comes from our immediate experience of life. We perceive and define freedom as 'the possibility to do what we want to do'.

If we want to be able to do something that we want to, we need two things:

1. The capability (physical and mental) to do it

2. The opportunity to exercise that action.

Freedom in that sense can be understood as:

- The ability to do something

- The absence of hindrance so that we can indeed move as we wish.

For instance: I want to drive my car from town A to town B. I know how to drive and I know the way. There is however an obstacle: the road is flooded. That means that in spite of my ability to do what I want to do, I am not at liberty to do it. I am blocked.

There is no doubt that freedom in this first and immediate sense (let's call it 'Freedom of movement') is a necessary condition for the implementation of our PTL. That makes it extremely valuable. Without it we are in pain and scared: when I lose my possibility to act and do things, my PTL is seriously jeopardised.

Question

Back to your notes. Where do you stand now regarding the arguments presented so far?

Let's examine now two more fundamental levels of freedom that are and have always been the subject of heated debates: the freedom to want what we want (generally referred to as 'free will') and the freedom to decide how to act in order to accomplish what we want ('freedom of decision').

We shall now address these two important levels of freedom before concluding on how free we ultimately are to accomplish our PTL in full.

First, the illusion of 'free will'.

This is a traditional metaphysical issue that has always given, and continues to give, grounds for endless discussion. It can be formulated as follows: 'I am free to decide what I want to do' rather than 'I am free to do what I have decided', as implied in the freedom of movement mentioned above.

To put it more simply, we could say, 'Am I at liberty to want or not to want to do something evil, to tell the truth or not, to lust or not for my neighbour's wife or husband?'

In other words, does there indeed exist such an upstream degree of freedom that would be called the 'free will', and which would open the possibility that we could decide on our will itself or to choose between two or several forms of will?

The clear answer given by the PTL model to this crucial question is *no*! No, because our primordial will, our first motive, our driving desire is set in us right from the start: it is our Will-to-Live! Therefore, every time we want something, we know this aspiration will directly derive from our will to perpetuate our existence. We are not free to decide whether we accept this primordial will or not: if we don't accept it we die! (But even in such a case, which is what is called suicide, we shall see that we don't really counter our Will-to-Live). So we can say at this stage that any wish or desire that we have is simply generated by our Will-to-Live. There is not much we can do about it, except decide not to satisfy it because of a stronger desire that will tell us, 'Don't do that if you want to favour your PTL! There are better ways to fulfil your Will-to-Live!'

Question
Does it upset you to know that there is no such a thing as 'free will'?

Second, the freedom of decision.

Given that we can't decide what we want (that is, initially to go on living, and consequently all the series of things that we need to satisfy this initial aspiration), the next question is, 'Can we freely decide on what we should do to best satisfy the needs of our PTL?'

The answer is yes in appearance, but not really...! Using our rational and analytical abilities, we can indeed explore our internal and external options to reflect and decide on what's best for our Project-to-Live.

We must however realise that the decision process is pre-conditioned by the pressure coming from the Will-to-Live (we must do and be what's in the interest of our PTL), and by the givens of our Power-to-Live (we can only think within the framework of our Power Map).

So it seems that the freedom of decision or choice can apparently be exercised, but only within a set of pre-established givens:

We can scan the nature and structure of our Power Map and decide on what we want to activate, use and improve so that we are indeed in good shape PTL-wise. But our Power Map is already there, as well as our ability to scan it (which is in fact also part of it...)

We can look around, probe and explore the environment (also part of our Power Map...) to spot some new means that we could use to our advantage, but again this is nothing else than making use of and changing our already existing Power Map.

What freedom are we thus finally left with?

Here is what we can and cannot do according to the PTL model:

- Cannot do
  - Decide on the purpose of life (there is no such thing as free will)
  - Think and decide outside our predetermined parameters.

- Can do
  - Maximise the use of the parts of our Power Map that we think serve our PTL best
  - Identify other means and learn how to use them and eventually acquire them in order to enhance the quality of our PTL.

Finally, it seems that what makes us different from the other species is not, as has often been put forward, our autonomy and ability to decide in a free way, but rather our faculty to think. This allows us to understand ourselves as projects and project at a distance in space and time the consequences of our acts.

2. Am I responsible?

The question here is the following: Are we responsible for our deeds in this world, or, in other words, can we be held accountable for what we do to others and to ourselves? A big question! And one that we should not answer too quickly...

Let's remember what we said earlier: there is no such thing as 'free will'. We are predetermined to do all that we do – predetermined by our Will-to-Live which pushes us forward, and by our Power Map, which makes us who we are, with our strengths and weaknesses, our ability to think and judge, our capability to make decisions. When we act, we act to the best of our judgement in the best interests of our PTL. It was Socrates that once said that no man ever chooses evil deliberately...

So if we are predetermined, how can we be held answerable for what we do? And yet, let's face it, the notion of responsibility is ingrained in our thinking, in our values, everywhere in the world. So how can this paradox be resolved?

Let's start by addressing the notion of responsibility as it is generally understood. Most of the time, we tend to consider a person responsible for what he or she did if:

- He/she was not forced by an 'external' power (another person, or natural circumstances) to act as she did, and

- He/she was conscious of the eventual consequences of her act.

In other words, a person is considered responsible if he or she acts deliberately, of his/her own volition and is in possession of his/her senses.

Now, if we were strictly rational, we would say that this is inconsistent with our negation of 'free will': it's not fair to consider someone responsible, if we stress at the same time that that person was not 'free' to act differently anyway. Yes, strictly speaking, this is true, and therefore we should not consider 'responsibility' as making sense at all, at least from a philosophical standpoint.

This kind of reasoning, incidentally, very often results in people being disconcerted and sometimes even angry. They will say, 'If we are not responsible for our deeds, then we might as well do whatever we please and no one will hold it against us!' Well, this is simply a wrong extrapolation! Indeed, the ultimate reference and interest that everybody has in mind is his or her PTL. So we will never tend to do 'whatever we please' without considering the impact that such an action will have at the end of the day on our own existence. If I hurt someone else, he or she might well hit back. If I am benevolent, I will probably get some form of reward in return. And hence this brings us back to the conventionally accepted sense of responsibility as we will now describe it.

For we are living in a social, practical world where we interact with others, and that is how we have developed this idea of responsibility. Indeed, we need that notion to set limits on our mutual conduct and the consequences it can have on our respective PTLs. Therefore, without even considering the aspect of 'free will' to its full philosophical extent, we will say the following: as long as a person responds to the two conditions mentioned above (acting deliberately, possessing one's senses and without being coerced by an external force) that person will be regarded as answerable, which will authorise me to either praise her or condemn her. That's the social convention mankind has generally adopted, as we said for practical purposes; but as anyone can quickly conclude, it remains paradoxical, since it obliterates the fact that no one is really 'free', and fuzzy, since it is hard to decide when somebody acted in his 'senses', 'deliberately' and without any outside constraint. Because of this fuzziness, responsibility is almost always a case of endless debate, both in people's consciences and in courts of law.

By the way, we should also emphasise that responsibility, as just described, applies to our being accountable not only to others but also to ourselves; indeed, we very often pass judgements on our own behaviour, blaming or praising ourselves for what we have done.

RESPONSIBILITY AND EMOTIONS

There are many emotions that are tied to our sense of 'responsibility'. If we consider that we have acted appropriately (in line with the interests of our PTL), we feel good and confident about ourselves. If we think that we have done wrong, we feel badly and regret our action. Now this is quite understandable, since our emotions reflect something that has happened to our PTL and affects its accomplishment one way or the other.

Such emotions are also useful because they reflect an evaluation we make of our deeds, from which we can learn. If we feel positively we will remember that the way we have acted is to be retained and repeated in similar circumstances. And so vice versa. That's how we can learn to improve our behaviour and become more effective in accomplishing our PTL.

But while such emotions are indeed healthy and useful, they can take a pathological turn when they become too strong and irrational: then instead of 'confidence' we might feel 'vanity', and instead of 'regret' we could feel 'guilt'. This is too much, since we should always remember that at the end of the day we are not really responsible for what we did, but predetermined by who we are... Therefore the 'healthy' attitude is to learn from our successes or mistakes and change 'who we are', i.e. our Power-to-Live, accordingly, knowing that these newly integrated lessons will help to determine our conduct in the future.

3. How can I cope with the tragic side of my existence?

All decisions imply a sacrifice on our part. The exercise of our responsibility (despite the lack of 'free will'), the determination of our behaviours, the accomplishment of our PTL, the handling of conflicting notions, the struggle between entertainment and work, the short-term benefit versus the long-term one, the conflict between my PTL and the social code of conduct are all loaded with dilemmas, paradoxes and dramas.

Our lives are full of tradeoffs. We must compromise, weigh the pros and cons of the various options which are available and then, decide. We must give away parts of our Power-to-Live in order to acquire the new ones that we think we need to move on successfully.

Question

What parts of your Power Map are you ready to give away?

We get nothing for nothing. The functioning of our PTL requires those sacrifices. It is the challenge of being alive. We must choose to go ahead. It is inherent to our essence. We struggle.

This is what we call the tragic dimension of life. Nobody is spared. To live is to experience it. Life is risky.

Note, however, that in practice we identify this tragic aspect only in decisions that have a significant impact on our life. Not in the multitude of small decisions and petty choices that we make daily.

We consider tragic a situation that implies a decision on our part that clearly appears as being capable of impacting our PTL in a serious way.

In this sense we think it useful to distinguish between the concepts of 'tragic' and 'dramatic'.

Tragic: is when we have to decide between two or more possible ways to accomplish our PTL. A decision of this kind implies the necessity of giving up an advantage or taking a risk or accepting an evil as a reduction of our Power-to-Live.

Dramatic: is the actual harmful impact that our decisions (or any external event) can have on our PTL. A tragic situation is thus full of potential dramatic consequences.

The sign of tragedy marks every crossroads of our life. We are really facing a tragedy when we are facing a decision that carries heavy dramatic consequences.

Ethical choices are very often the source of tragedies in people's lives.

A powerful example of a tragedy is the story of Antigone. Antigone had to choose between 1) obeying the King (Creon) and forgoing the last sacred rites due to her brother, who died whilst battling against Creon; or 2) going by the gods' rules and prescriptions, and burying her brother in a way that would ensure him eternal peace, but then being sentenced to death by Creon. Antigone faces a tragic decision: either way she loses!

Question

Have you ever experienced something tragic in your life? Do you remember what it was? Would you say it was tragic, or dramatic?

4. Is courage the answer?

What is courage then? What are the main characteristics of somebody who is courageous?

THE REAL MEANING OF COURAGE

Before we go to the usual ways of referring to courage, let us just define the real meaning of the concept. Courage is essentially a judgement passed on one's behaviour by a third person. I will not consider myself as courageous whatever I do, for the simple reason that if I do something, however difficult, painful, risky that act may be, I do it because I consider that it's the best way to serve my PTL. But someone else observing me might think, 'I would never have done that...' or, 'I'm not sure I would have done it, because of the negatives implied. He or she must be very courageous to have chosen that course of action.' In other words, we talk of courage when we consider another person's actions, wondering whether we would have decided to do the same thing, when in fact that person only did it because he or she thought there was no better way to accomplish his or her PTL!

Now let's look at people's ways of being 'courageous'.

There are many different ways to look at courage:

- The courage to own one's own life
- The courage to face the tragedies of one's own life
- The courage to give one's own life away.

THE COURAGE TO OWN ONE'S LIFE

It is, in a way, much easier to give up the ownership of one's own life to somebody or something else:

- God
- The State
- My father

- Luck
- Other people.

It is simpler. It is, in a way, more comforting ('My life is to serve Christ and enjoy swimming'). It makes sense because it eliminates a series of important questions about one's self, origins and destiny. It takes the anguish away.

If all the answers are in the 'book', and the code of conduct has been set up in advance and by a transcendent source, then life becomes much more straightforward. We go by the book and, we are 'saved'.

It does require courage, not to reject the 'book' altogether, but to accept accountability for one's own existence. I am what I am, and I must do the best that I can do with what I have got from nature and education. I own my life.

We need courage to cope with questions such as, 'Where are we coming from? Where are we going? Why do we exist? What is the meaning of my life? Why the pain? Why the suffering?'

We need courage to accept that there is no such thing as 'free will'!

Courage is useful if we want to pursue the exploration of our essence at the risk of discovering that there are no answers, that those questions are irrelevant or that the answers are predetermined.

THE COURAGE TO FACE THE TRAGEDIES AND DRAMAS OF ONE'S OWN LIFE

We do suffer. We suffer tremendously when the vital elements of our PTL are affected by the circumstances of our life. We cannot avoid it. We all:

- Die
- See loved ones die
- Get sick and lose our health
- Get old and become incapacitated
- Have to compromise with some basic values to survive
- Fail
- Hurt others and make them suffer.

It is sometimes unbearable. And yet, life goes on...

We need strength and will to cope, fight and... accept. We must be able to mobilise our energy and patience (as well as our 'wisdom') to go on and still accomplish our PTL in the best possible way.

The courage to give one's own life away...

5. Is suicide an option?

Some people go as far as sacrificing themselves for the sake of others. How do we explain this behaviour, which is apparently in contradiction with the PTL model?

Is this self-sacrificing behaviour the exception to the rule? Is it the ultimate courageous act – to renounce our essence and Will-to-Live? Do we have that power?

If the answer to the above question is 'yes', then do we have the 'free will' that we denied ourselves before...?

Question

How do you answer that question?

Our answer is negative! No, we do not have that option. To give our life away is still an act in line with our PTL. In a way, it has nothing to do with courage.

We give our lives for two main reasons:

1. For self-serving reasons
2. Because of our identification with others.

Let's examine those two statements one at a time.

FOR SELF-SERVING REASONS

We claim that a moral act is rarely, if ever, pure in the sense that it totally excludes self-interest. Therefore we can hardly avoid considering selfishness as a possible motive behind the 'heroic' behaviour which consists in giving one's own life for the sake of another human being (or many people).

By sacrificing my life for another human being, I may very well find a personal satisfaction that is primarily related to my PTL. This satisfaction will lie essentially in the positive feeling towards me that my sacrifice will raise among others. By giving my life, I expect to receive in exchange admiration, respect and fame. If, in addition, I happen to believe in a future life, then I will probably also expect some kind of recognition in the next world... My PTL will exist for ever!

But what is the value, one might object, of such a glory, if it can only be granted to me in exchange for my life? What good is a posthumous fame if I am not around to enjoy it? How is it conceivable that I would give up what is for me the highest value, my PTL, in favour of a satisfaction which in any case can only be estimated in terms of how it contributes (maybe) to that very Project-to-Live.

The answer is: It seems that the admiration that the self-sacrificing act will give to the 'hero' is more predominant in his imagination than the fear of his or her death that is the price of it. And whilst the hero is still alive and is contemplating his forthcoming sacrifice, he paradoxically feels infinitely reinforced in his Power-to-Live by the love and admiration of others. In other words, the hero is on a high. He or she is overwhelmed with extremely positive emotions that support the heroic act. He has the impression, however short-lived it may be, of possessing an immortal potential. This is undoubtedly what often happens when a soldier deliberately and heroically gives his life up to protect his comrades in war. And let's also consider that the argument can be reversed. Some people will act heroically because they cannot stand the idea that if they do not do so they will be despised by others for having preferred their own survival to the lives of comrades that they could have saved.

FOR IDENTIFICATION WITH OTHERS

Let's remember that one of the principal causes of moral behaviour is the intrinsic capacity of our imagination to assimilate the Will-to-Live of other living beings with our own. There are times when we believe that by serving their PTL we are also contributing to our own.

Let's observe here that some people go as far as giving their lives away because they confuse their own existences with others' and are not able to distinguish their own PTL from others' any more. This can lead to the noblest of disinterested sacrifices: 'I will help my fellow being, whatever it costs me, because I cannot stand to see her suffer. When she suffers, I feel it in my own PTL as if it were me suffering!'

But this can be very pathological and lead to extreme manipulation by some dangerous individuals (dictators, sect leaders and fanatics). This phenomenon has been well studied, especially in connection with the so-called crowd manifestations or mass movements. Some people have apparently a strong need to identify themselves with the leaders in order to function properly and effectively. It is part of their Power Map. They must be led. They will make the ultimate sacrifice because of their need to be recognised as faithful followers and servers.

There are people who will accept death to accomplish the PTL that they identify with the most. They will do it because they perceive the other person's PTL of greater value and more worthy than their own.

The 'other' element can be:

- A group of persons that my sacrifice will save. In this case, it is the multiplying factor (more PTLs will survive) which leads to my self-sacrificing behaviour. All those PTLs together have a greater value than my own single Will-to-Live. We see here the danger of such a self-demeaning way of valuing one's own PTL... Heroism is perhaps not always so great after all.

  The classical example is a prisoner of war who will refuse to give any information about his comrades at the risk of losing his life because he sees a greater value of life in the group he can save and with which he identifies than in his own single PTL.

- The 'other' person is a child or someone much younger or healthier than I am. If I find myself in a situation where I can exchange my life for his, I could be inclined to do it for the reason that his PTL will appear to me as having more potential for life than my own and therefore can be favourably substituted for mine.

Let's not lose sight of the fact that if I envisage putting into question my own existence, it is only because I replace it through identification by one or several other existences. By doing so, it is as if my own PTL got absorbed into others and to its own advantage (some religions have used this identification phenomenon for their own sake!).

Self-sacrificing is still an act of life...

Question

Do you agree with the above arguments? If not, what is your own position regarding the question of self-sacrifice? List your arguments.

- Is suicide an option?

- Why do people commit suicide? The delicate (and yet fundamental) question that we must then answer is:

- Is suicide an invalidation of the PTL model?

If our PTL has no other purpose than its own perpetuation, then suicide obviously appears as an irrefutable invalidation of this assertion.

If, again, we have no other will than to survive, how come so many people end up taking their own lives? This is indeed a vital question.

We do not deny that suicide does at first sight constitute an intriguing and paradoxical behaviour. It is a direct provocation towards a philosophical mode that claims that life tends in every instance to ensure its preservation.

How can we reconcile this contradiction?

It is possible to rationally resolve this apparent *faux pas* of the Will-to-Live. Actually, we believe that the decision to commit suicide is not only compatible with the will to preserve one's own existence but even that it confirms the absolute predominance of the Project-to-Live.

But before going further, let's have a look at 'death'.

What is death? Death is, by definition, the annihilation of our PTL. It is the end of its implementation. It means that we do not exist any more.

What is fascinating about the concept (and the reality) of death is that nobody has ever been conscious of being dead, for death implies precisely the loss of one's conscience. Death is not something that we can experience first hand. In fact, we are aware of death only under the form of an abstraction or construction of the mind. Of course, our ideas about death are also related to extrapolations of the negative events of our life (our imagination) and also the observing of what happens to other living beings when they experience what we have called 'death'.

In both cases, this all leads to a projection of our fantasy: either we imagine our PTL as being inapt to exist any longer or we identify ourselves with some other being whose PTL has ceased to be.

Let's repeat: as long as we are alive, our PTL is ongoing and when we die we are no longer in a position to acknowledge its cessation. Or to quote the famous saying of the Latin poet, Lucretius: 'Where I am, death is not; and where death is not, I am not.'

Life presents the particular aspect that as long as it dynamically expands it cannot picture its own absolute negation.

Let's review two typical, but not exclusive, categories of suicide: the first, which is the most frequent, is where suicide is caused by *despair*; and the second, more exceptional, when it is motivated by self-sacrifice for the sake of *love*.

SUICIDE DUE TO DESPAIR

Let's first analyse the behaviour of a person who wants to put an end to his or her life because it has become unbearable.

The key to such behaviour lies precisely in the fact that for that individual life has become *unbearable*.

What does that notion of unbearable mean?

Unbearable is what is contrary to life. If I feel that my life can no longer be endured, it is because it appears to me that it can no longer respond to its purpose, which is to perpetuate my existence. In other words, the desperate person is the person who *feels that he or she is dying*, meaning that he/she feels that the negative forces which weigh on his/her Power-to-Live are prevailing over the latter's capacity to confront them. He/she feels there is no hope any more. He/she despairs.

A person who perceives that his or her PTL is incurably jeopardised and moving towards its own annihilation experiences despair.

It is the most terrible thing which can happen to any living being: feeling powerless before the shrinking of one's Power-to-Live and therefore the very negation of one's Will-to-Live.

It matters little what the circumstances are which produce such a situation or which part of the Power-to-Live they have impacted. What counts is the suffering that is perceived, the impression that one's PTL is irrevocably in check. There is no hope. 'I have no way out.' I despair...

Again, nothing, by virtue of the very definition of the PTL, can be more painful for any human being than the feeling of dying, losing one's Power-to-Live. Not even death itself can be more excruciating. Here lies the key to the explanation of suicide.

We must understand that people who choose to kill themselves do it not because they prefer death to life (however painful the latter may be for them) but rather because death (as a concept) appears to them *less contrary to life* than the very impression of dying (felt as a reality) which at that particular moment marks their existence.

Let's say it again: they select death because it is less intolerable than the feeling of a disappearing Power-to-Live.

Again, how is this possible?

Because death, as we mentioned above, is not for us a reality but only a projection of our imagination. None of us has ever experienced death! We therefore do not know it. We can speculate about it. We still do not have a good grasp of it. However frightful death can seem to be (at least in our representation of it), it can never be as repulsive as the impression of dying.

To put it differently, it looks as if our suffering can reach a degree where it reflects a state which is more contrary to our Project-to-Live than the abstract idea of death that our imagination has extrapolated from its observations and learning.

So we see death, at such terrible moments, as a way (and even the only possible way) of escaping our pain. We will favour death against the unbearable ordeal we are facing at that time in our life.

Since we are governed by our Will-to-Live, there are times in our lives when we would rather be dead than to feel ourselves dying. It is so because the abstract representation of death that I have in mind seems more remote, less real than the immediate sensation that I have that my life is abandoning me.

By committing suicide, I resort to virtual death in order to escape real death.

As one commits suicide, the act of dying (which will be chosen to be as quick and painless as possible) should hardly be felt at all in comparison with the relief expected from death itself. The issue is not about opposing one suffering to another but to put an end to the actual suffering that one is enduring by an act of deliverance.

We can thus conclude that suicide due to despair does not in any way contradict the PTL model. It can on the contrary be viewed as an illustration of the absolute prevalence of our Will-to-Live.

SUICIDE FOR THE SAKE OF LOVE

This second category of suicides is generally considered as the most sublime form of individual behaviour insofar as it represents the ultimate moral act.

How can somebody just give his or her life to another person for the sake of love? Can we explain (using the PTL model) why a person will commit suicide on the basis of the feelings that he or she has towards another individual?

Here again, we'll find the two basic foundations of the PTL explanation. People do sacrifice themselves through love for:

- selfish reasons
- reasons of identification.

Selfish reasons

The fact that I love the other means that I judge that he or she is good for me and therefore favours my PTL. Thus, the more I love the other person, the more she counts for me and the more I will be inclined to protect her PTL.

If I become aware that this other person that I love is threatened in her own existence, this causes me pain for I feel that I am myself in danger of losing her.

The more the person is dear to me and the more I will be afraid of the risk of losing her. It could well happen that I am so attached to that person (who is indispensable for the conduct of my own existence) that her loss will appear to me as absolutely unbearable.

I will then find myself in the situation described previously regarding suicide due to despair. Nothing will seem to me as more unendurable than this suffering that I am anticipating by losing the beloved one, including my own death.

Reasons of identification

In this case, it is not only the loss of the cherished one that leads us to our sacrifice but the perspective of undergoing her suffering or dying as if we were ourselves that other person.

It is suicide for love with an additional dimension, which is that we identify with the other person as if she were us and therefore feel her ordeal all the more severely.

Question

Have you ever encountered people who talked about committing suicide, and who then did it? Does it fit with what we said before?

What are the leadership implications?

Let's start with the 'easy' one: If I'm not free, then what?

Frankly speaking, it doesn't make any difference in the way you should operate!

You will function with the Power-to-Live that you have and which determines you, and you will be responsible for what you do anyway, because people around you who have given you a mandate to lead the business sector that is under your jurisdiction will hold you accountable for your results.

So just be who you are. If you are successful, feel the increase in your self-esteem (without becoming vain, if possible...); and if you make mistakes, don't blame yourself, just draw the right conclusions and take corrective action.

Five questions leaders must answer one way or another:

1.   As a leader, do you feel responsible for:

   •   Your own decisions and actions

   •   The consequences of your actions on your team members

   •   Activating the main elements of your Power-to-Live through your leadership role

   •   Fulfilling your PTL

   •   Helping others to feel responsible for their own PTL?

2.   Are you sure that being a leader is really what you need to fulfil your PTL?

3.   How good are you at coping with the dramatic and tragic dimensions of human lives (yours as well as your team members')?

4.   How do you assess your ability to take risks for the sake of your PTL?

5. How far do you go in encouraging people to take risks for the sake of their PTLs?

We do not think to understand, but to make the world manageable for our use.

Nietzsche

10. Putting my life in order

What is it?

This is about putting the key pieces of the PTL model together, summarising it and having a good look at how it can be used. It is about the art of living. The art of:

- Making sense of our own life
- Taking the right decisions for the sake of our life
- Owning what we are.

Keep in mind that if you are interested, and if you have not done it yet, there is a test on this topic in the second part of the book. The journal (Part III of the book) also aims at helping you to review the 'management' of your life using the PTL model.

What's in it for me?

You will get a chance to review the PTL model and its key components. We will show you how it works in practice and what can be learned from its implementation. A practical set of guidelines will be presented in the next pages for your own use. This is the ultimate step in trying to 'convince' you, the reader, that our approach can make sense and help you live a better life.

Philosophy can indeed contribute in a very pragmatic way to the conduct of your existence. What do you have to lose?

What is the red thread?

We'll first have a look at:

1. The model: All-in-One
2. Guidelines on the art of living

Then we'll move on and examine:

    3. A short illustration of the model at work

    4. A quiz to check your understanding

    5. Questions for your day-to-day life.

1. The model: All-in-One

The Project-to-Live (PTL) model is a philosophical approach to life. It aims at helping us live a better life. It has three key ingredients, i.e. the Will-to-Live, the Power-to-Live and the Way-to-Live.

THE WILL-TO-LIVE

This is the fundamental driver, which exists in all living beings and determine all our behaviours.

It has only one objective: the perpetuation of life ('We exist to live').

Two measurements can be made in relation to the Will-to-Live:

- The Vitality Quotient (VQ) which assesses the intensity (energy level) of the Will-to-Live (see Part II of the book).

- The Emotional Quotient (EQ) which tells us how well we are doing in relation to our PTL and its fundamental intent, which is to live (see Part II of the book).

THE POWER-TO-LIVE

The Power-to-Live is made up of all the elements of the world that we can use to fulfil our primary objective, which is to live.

The recognition and use of all the ingredients of the world (internal and external, acquired and innate, conscious and unconscious) is what makes us unique and different ('I am the world').

Each individual has a personal (again unique) way of going about accomplishing his or her Project-to-Live. It is a fabulous challenge that all of us have to pick up.

Two dimensions must be taken into account if we want to manage our PTL properly:

- The individual Power Map (my way to ensure the success of my PTL).

- Other people's Power Maps (their ways to accomplish their PTL).

THE WAY-TO-LIVE

The Way-to-Live is made up of all our behaviours and actions. Everything that we do to ensure the perpetuation of our life. This is the PTL in action.

It includes essentially two notions:

- Action, composed of: work (as the activation and development of our vital functions); and entertainment (or the activities we get involved in to avoid boredom or simply to intensify our life).

- Emotions (as the signals that our PTL sends back to itself to indicate where it stands with regard to its own accomplishment).

Also, there are the two important combined elements of:

- Responsibility
- Ownership.

They are part of our behaviour (Way-to-Live), and reflect our understanding of and attitude towards our PTL.

2. Guidelines on the art of living

Here is a 'checklist' that you can use to take stock of your life and make decisions (better hopefully) on your next actions.

Ten PTL guidelines to assess and improve the quality of your life:

CHECKPOINT 1: THE REFERENCE

Description:

This is the foundation of the PTL model approach. There is no meaning without a reference. Human beings cannot survive, function, act or achieve anything without relating to some kind of reference in order to understand what's happening within and without themselves and other individuals.

Motto:

No reference... no meaning!

Ten guidelines:

1. Take the time to sit down from time to time and ask yourself what's the meaning of everything you do. Do it now!

2. Check on your reference right now (What is it? Are you happy about it?).

3. Measure the impact of your reference on the quality of your life (do it by listening to your emotions).

4. More specifically, look at the impact of your fundamental reference on the way you think, feel and behave.

5. Identify some of the key intermediary references that you use to live your private and professional life.

6. Assess your ability to know, understand and accept (and learn from) the references of the people close to you.

7. Be aware of the problems, difficulties and challenges due to the discrepancy between your ultimate reference (the PTL) and the requirements of the situation you are in right now.

8. Explore some of the implications (for you) of accepting the Will-to-Live as the only reference.

9. Examine how the PTL model (as a core reference) can help you live a better life.

10. List all the personal advantages you can get out of a non-transcendental reference.

CHECKPOINT 2: KNOWLEDGE

Description:

The critical components of knowledge are data/information/wisdom (and creed for the believers). The creation of knowledge is a vital process. It involves three key questions:

1. How does the physical world tie together? (Science)

2. What does it mean for me? (Experience)
3. Why does it mean what it means? (Philosophy)

Motto:

To know is to invent one's reality.

Ten guidelines:

1. Be aware of the assumptions ('facts' that you take for granted) that you use to run your life.
2. Do check your assumptions from time to time.
3. Check on how good you are at transforming facts into something meaningful for you (and others).
4. Consider the following question: What does life mean for us as human beings?
5. Talk to others about your interpretations of the meaning of 'things'.
6. Have a good look at your position regarding religion and God as the source of all meanings.
7. Improve your tolerance of ambiguity (see test in Part II).
8. Challenge facts.
9. Put things into perspective.
10. Make sure that you never forget that you do not know (Socrates).

CHECKPOINT 3: THE VITALITY QUOTIENT

Description:

The Vitality Quotient (VQ) can be used to measure how intensely activated your PTL is. It is about your energy level and the intensity with which you live your life. The VQ is also about:

- your stamina and your ability to live up to your high life expectations
- your ability to energise yourself and others
- your capacity to face the tragedies of your life with strength and stoicism.

Motto:

The Will-to-Live is the engine of life and energy is its fuel.

Ten guidelines:

1. Know your VQ (see test in Part II).
2. Measure your ability at mobilising your energy when it is necessary.
3. Decide on what you want, i.e. intensity or duration in your life.
4. Use your energy to promote your PTL.
5. Learn how to energise others.
6. Spot some practical ways to improve your VQ.
7. Grow from your personal ways of coping with the ups and downs of your life.
8. Stop from time to time and 'recharge your batteries'.
9. Use boredom as a challenge to expand and develop.
10. Believe in yourself and in your ability to be 'successful'.

CHECKPOINT 4: THE EMOTIONAL QUOTIENT

Description:

Emotions are the dashboard of our PTL. They tell us what shape our Project-to-Live is in. Emotions, with their constituents, sensations and feelings, inform us about the status (at a certain point in time) of our life. They are the indispensable tools that must be used to check on the good or bad implementation of our PTL. They can also help us assess the values of the very components of our Power-to-Live. Happiness and unhappiness tell us something about the parts of the Power Map that we care about.

Motto:

Emotions are the language of the Project-to-Live.

Ten guidelines:

1. Acknowledge the important role played by emotions in your life.

2. Check on your ability to handle your own emotions.

3. Monitor your emotions on a regular basis.

4. Watch and learn from other people's emotions.

5. Ask the people whom you trust to help you understand your emotions.

6. Identify the link between your current emotions and your PTL.

7. Know what gives you great happiness and learn from it.

8. Know what gives you great unhappiness and learn from it.

9. Assess your ability to love and hate.

10. Pinpoint what creates fear and hope in you.

CHECKPOINT 5: THE INDIVIDUAL POWER MAP

Description:

The individual Power Map is what makes somebody behave this way rather than that. It is what makes you unique. It is the set of means that any human being prefers using to fulfil his or her PTL. It is what differentiates one person from another. It is made up of the 'objects' of the world (tangible and intangible) arranged in a specific personal fashion. It is what makes human life exciting. It is the Power Map with its preservation and expansion that gives us the challenge in our life.

Motto:

'I am the world.'

Ten guidelines:

1. Recognise the existence and importance of your Power Map.

2. Make an inventory of the essentials of your Power Map.

3. Compare your Power Map with other people's.

4. Know what your Power Map's best assets (priorities) are.

5. Set up a plan to expand your Power Map (or take full advantage of it).

6. Concentrate on using the most valued parts of your Power Map.

7. Identify potential conflicts between your Power Map and the organisation you are working for.

8. Decide on what you would like to change in your Power Map.

9. Identify and analyse the Power Maps of the members of your family (or your friends).

10. Understand the Power Maps of the people you are working for.

CHECKPOINT 6: WORK

Description:

Work is (according to the PTL model) the activation of all our vital functions, i.e. body and mind!

It is the main way for us human beings to fulfil our Project-to-Live and ensure the accomplishment of the Will-to-Live.

Through work we carry out our PTL, use the different elements of our Power-to-Live and expand our possibilities to grow. Through work we become what we want and are deep down inside.

If we stop working, we get into trouble. Without work we basically 'shrink', and our PTL becomes more and more vulnerable.

Work is what makes us alive. It is vital for our balance and development. There are two alternatives to work. They are rest and entertainment.

Motto:

'To live is to work and to work is to live.'

Ten guidelines:

1. Come up with your own definition of work.

2. Compare your definition with ours.

3. Monitor the activation of your vital functions.

4. Decide on how you can be more involved in life.

5. Know what your most fulfilling vital functions are.

6. Act on what you could/should change in your life to make work more meaningful and exciting.

7. Check if your job is giving you a fair chance to activate your PTL.

8. Identify three key components of your job, which are critical for your PTL.

9. Check on the emotions that you are experiencing at work. (What are they telling you about the present activation of your vital functions?)

10. Envisage the possibility of doing something else (with your private and professional life) more in line with your deep (PTL) aspirations.

CHECKPOINT 7: ENTERTAINMENT

Description:

Entertainment is what we do when we do not have an opportunity to work or activate our vital PTL functions, or when we want to intensify our impression of living. It does not bring anything concrete to the realisation of our PTL and yet it can be quite useful.

It gives us an opportunity to relax from time to time and 'recharge our batteries' without falling into boredom, or to feel good just by stimulating our Power-to-Live. Or it provides us the pleasure of feeling that we are functioning (living) intensely.

It is important however to be aware that too much entertainment is debilitating because it uses up energy and parts of our Power-to-Live without adding any value to our PTL.

Motto:

'Entertainment is not life but an illusion of life.'

Ten guidelines:

1. Identify your most valued hobby.

2. Understand what you get out of your hobby.

3. Allow yourself to celebrate your efforts (and hopefully successes) from time to time.

4. Assess your overall position regarding entertainment.

5. Be aware of how you use the so-called free time in your life.

6. Know what bores you.

7. Know why you are pushing yourself to the limit (if that is the case).

8. Define what a waste of time means for you.

9. Know when to stop, slow down and when to work.

10. Manage your time so that you have a good balance between work and entertainment.

CHECKPOINT 8: ETHICS

Description:

Ethics are a code of conduct. They are a set of accepted norms of behaviour. They are also made up of values. Ethics are short cuts to decision making. They are a repertoire of more or less ready-made answers, which facilitate life, especially social relations.

Without ethics we would have to ponder each decision to make sure that it is good for our PTL and for our relations with others. With ethics we have automatic (and yet flexible) answers to our daily challenges. Our ethical code is part of our Power-to-Live.

Motto:

'Ethics are a guide for living a better life.'

Ten guidelines:

1. Be first aware of the fact that your way of thinking and behaving is largely predetermined by your code of ethics.

2. List ten behaviours which are part of your personal code of ethics.

3. Measure the flexibility of your code of conduct.

4. Review it from time to time.

5. Identify and understand other people's code of ethics.

6. Challenge your basic assumptions about ethics.

7. Learn how to solve the conflicts between various codes of ethics.

8. Be aware of the code of ethics in your organisation. List

some of its key characteristics.

9. Check if your ethics match your company's and act accordingly.

10. More important, own your code of conduct.

CHECKPOINT 9: RESPONSIBILITY

Description:

Responsibility is linked to commitment and accountability. It is about ownership: Who is ultimately in charge?

Who is responsible for my PTL?

This is about freedom and free will!

It raises the fundamental question of who controls my life and how.

We have seen that the Will-to-Live doesn't allow us free will. We are driven by it. We have no choice but to live. We also know that most of our behaviours are also determined by the demands of the Power-to-Live. We'll always do what we believe is 'right' for our PTL. We are not free! And yet... we own our life. Through the use and development of our Power-to-Live we take charge. We play and make every effort to be the maximum of what we can be. We empower ourselves!

Motto:

'I own what I am.'

Ten guidelines:

1. Start by feeling in charge of your Project-to-Live.

2. Identify what your boundaries are.

3. Know who you are and take charge.

4. Own your private life.

5. Own your professional life.

6. Stand up for what you are.

7. Acknowledge your strengths.

8. Recognise your weaknesses.

9. Do not allow anybody to own your life.

10. Optimise the use of everything you have.

CHECKPOINT 10: THE PROJECT-TO-LIVE (PTL)

Description:

The PTL is a philosophical model about life. It is a way of looking at ourselves, and can help me:

- Become more aware of what drives my life and me.
- Understand better why I am doing what I am doing (and how).
- Manage my life in a better way and maximise what I am.

It is made up of three key elements, i.e. the Will-to-Live, the Power-to-Live and the Way-to-Live.

Motto:

'I am a project, the project of my own perpetuation.'

Ten guidelines:

1. Perceive yourself as a project.
2. Identify the basic drive in yourself.
3. Know and understand your Will-to-Live.
4. Question your usual ways of giving meanings to 'things'.
5. Be ready to have a good look at yourself and take stock of your life.
6. Accept the proposition that there is no such a thing as 'free will'.
7. Take charge of your own life.
8. Be aware that there is no absolute way for us human beings to understand the world, and that knowledge is a tool that we use to manage our lives on this planet.
9. Listen to your emotions. They are important signals.
10. Make sure that you live at the top of your potential.

3. A short illustration of the model at work

Below is a very simple story about a person's PTL. Please read it and try to apply the model on that individual and her existence.

Keep two questions in mind while reading the short text:

1. What's wrong with Jane?
2. What do you think she should do?

ONE DAY IN JANE COLLINS' LIFE: A SCENARIO

It is Monday, 22 October 1998 in Paris, France. The time is 7.30 a.m.

Jane is in her kitchen getting ready to go to her new office in downtown Paris. She is reflecting on her three last months at WWR (an international organisation responsible for checking on the quality of water worldwide and managing projects for its improvement) and does not feel good about it.

Nothing is going the right way, she tells herself. Her emotions begin to take over as she looks back at the way she has been treated since her arrival in Paris in June 1998...

'We desperately need somebody like you,' her new boss had said. He was a Swedish man in his forties and in charge of the operational division for water testing. Then he had added, 'With your expertise, energy and entrepreneurial spirit we are going to change quite a few things around. God knows we need it!'

All words, thinks Jane while eating an American-style breakfast; she hasn't got used to the light French breakfast –coffee and croissants – to eat in the morning. All words. No deeds...

What a frustrating experience! And on top of it, Brian [her husband] has decided to stay in the USA and isn't here to help me sort it out! she says to herself.

At 8.15, she is en route to the office.

'I cannot understand why all those French people go to the office by car. Just look at the traffic jams! And those people shouting at each other... I can't even understand what they are saying. My goodness, they are talking to me! ...Yes, yes... I'll move on... What a country!' she mumbles to herself in her little car, on her way to another depressing day.

By 9.15 she is in her office.

She is talking to her secretary, a young Japanese lady, who has just given her a note signed by the director of another department (TASS) responsible for standardisation and controls.

'I do not believe this! Do you realise [she's very angry now] that that man, M Hernandez [the chief of the TASS department] has again vetoed my proposal for a new kit to test the quality of water more effectively and speedily. This was my second draft. I do not understand how those people function here. Let me tell you that in America, this would have been looked at and resolved in a matter of days. Here we are, still talking after three months, and we're going nowhere! I must see M Hensen [her direct manager] right away!'

At 11.45 she is in M Hensen's office.

JANE: Look, M Hensen, you told me to move on fast with the water kit proposal. I did it. I sent my proposal to you. You approved it. I gave it to M Hernandez [Head of TASS] who blocked it. I rewrote it. You said that it was much better. And now he has vetoed it again... I am lost. What do I do now?

HENSEN: Jane... be patient. You must understand, this organisation is very old and bureaucratic. There are many rules around. Things go slowly. Just keep pushing. We need you...

12.30 (at lunch with a French colleague).

JANE: I'm completely lost here... I cannot achieve anything. People are strange. They act as if they do not want to succeed. Help me to understand this, please.

COLLEAGUE: Jane, you must understand that you are in the middle of a political game. Hensen and Hernandez are playing power games around your project. You must be smart and—

JANE (*interrupting*): I am not here to play political games. I am here to do my job – quickly and well. I don't care about the politics.

COLLEAGUE: Maybe you should care. At least a little...

It is 3 p.m. and Jane is in her office. She has rewritten her proposal for the third time. She is very upset. At 4.30 she is in M Hernandez' office.

JANE: M Hernandez, here is the new version of my water kit proposal. M Hensen likes it very much. I think you are going to like it this time. Please read it, and if you have any questions I am entirely at your disposal to answer them.

M HERNANDEZ (*not even looking at her*): Thank you. I'll do that. But you know, I'm not convinced that we actually need a new water testing kit. The one that we have is working very well. I'll let you know.

At 5 p.m., all the offices are empty. Jane is still working.

JANE'S SECRETARY: Here is a short note from M Hernandez which says that your proposal is still unacceptable.

JANE (*distressed*): I don't believe this! What shall I do?

By 5.30, Jane is stuck in another traffic jam.

JANE: I am wasting my time here. I must go home. It will be my first failure!

Jane continues on her way, distressed and even more upset.

4. A quiz to check your understanding

Here is an application of the PTL grid on the short story just presented. Look at each item and check on your own understanding of the scenario (one tick for each right answer). Then, move to the short debriefing at the end of the quiz:

1. THE REFERENCE

It is clear that the key players in the little story are using different sub-references, i.e.

- For Jane, her job is everything.

- Hensen and Hernandez are bureaucrats. They think first about their careers.

Tick here if you got this right:

2. KNOWLEDGE

It is quite obvious that the people involved look at the same situation from different perspectives (the same situation means different things for the protagonists of the story):

- Jane: 'I must help them change... fast.'

- Hensen: 'We must change, but slowly.'

- Hernandez: 'Everything is fine.' (The status quo is OK.)

Tick here if you got it right:

3. VITALITY QUOTIENT (VQ)

- Jane is full of vitality and energy.

- Hensen and Hernandez much more subdued and low-key.

Tick here if you got it right:

4. INDIVIDUAL POWER MAPS

They are quite different:

- Jane wants to achieve and get personal recognition. She wants to be a good professional and succeed.

- Hensen wants peace and harmony. He wants to survive in the company.

- Hernandez wants power and the status quo. He does not want to change.

Tick here if you got it right:

5. WORK

- Jane is strong on doing. She concentrates on the activation of her vital functions related to her job. Her professional life is very important for her.

- Hensen is slow on action. His behaviour is cautious. He does not want to take risks. He is in a kind of slow motion mode.

- Hernandez resists change. He doesn't want to move. He wants to preserve his PTL, not to expand it. He is in a blocking mode.

Tick here if you got it right:

6. ETHICS

One comment on ethics: Jane's code of conduct is, because of her experience in the USA (private sector), confronted here with a code of conduct that is totally different (international public sector). She wants to move fast, get results and be recognised as a good professional. The WWR code of ethics is more in line with: 'Be careful, listen to the old-timers, do not rush, respect authority...'

Tick here if you got it right:

7. EMOTIONS

This is the critical step of the story analysis. We can learn a lot from the emotions expressed in the dialogues:

- Jane is frustrated, angry and depressed.

- Hensen is a bit afraid of Jane's actions.

- Hernandez believes that he is right anyway and is not going to concede anything. He feels under attack. He does not like Jane.

All the emotions presented in the story tell us something on the key elements of the characters' Power Maps (see point 4 above).

Tick here if you got it right:

8. RESPONSIBILITY AND OWNERSHIP

- Jane seems to feel personally responsible for what she does (it is her life).

- Hensen and Hernandez give the impression of living through their organisation.

Tick here if you got it right:

SCORING AND DEBRIEFING

- If you scored between 6 and 8: Congratulations – you have a very good understanding of the PTL model.

- If you scored between 3 and 5: You have a good grasp but not quite good enough. We suggest that you go back to the All-in-One part and read it again.

- If you scored between 0 and 2: Maybe this model is not for you after all...

5. Questions for your day-to-day life

Here are a few pointers that you can use to check on your PTL on a daily basis and then make the 'right' decisions to live 'a better life':

Three questions for the morning:

1. Think back to your dream last night. Is it telling you something about your life? Were any emotions involved in the dream? What are they telling you about where you stand with your life right now? Any desires?

2. Before starting the day, review your Power Map and identify three elements that you would like to activate during the day so that you are going to be happy today.

3. Challenge yourself, and using your 'desires' single out one new thing you intend to do during the day in order to grow and expand.

Three questions for the afternoon:

1. Take stock of your job (what you have been doing today) and decide if it gives you a fair chance to be energised and meet your life aspirations. Is what you are doing making sense for you?

2. Take a minute to assess your relationships with your working partners (boss, colleagues, and team members...) and examine how you could help each other with your respective (and different) PTL so that you all benefit from your working environment.

3. More importantly, perhaps, check how your organisation cares about its employees, and if it has created a meaningful and sustaining environment for yourself and your partners at work.

Three questions for the evening:

1. Have a good look at what happened during the day, check on your emotions and learn from them. Are you basically all right? Is anything seriously wrong? Any new discoveries about yourself? Any changes you think you should make to be happier?

2. Is there anything you should maybe change in your code of conduct (ethics) so as to have a better match between your Project-to-Live and your environment? Check on your values. What is important for you?

3. One more time, check your 'life dreams'. What do you want to do with your life? What can you do to own it?

Just food for thought...

What are the leadership implications?

Here is a systematic way to use the PTL model to make a leadership diagnosis, make sound decisions and act more effectively as a leader.

A THREE-STEP APPROACH TO PTL LEADERSHIP

Step 1. Start with emotions: It is a good way to start because emotions as we know now are indicators of where people stand regarding their PTLs (Happy, unhappy, mad, sad...)

Questions

What are your team members' (or your bosses', for that matter) emotions telling you about them and their lives? Is any clarification or action required?

Step 2. Look now at the VQ or the energy level of your team members as well as of the team as a whole.

Questions

Is the VQ low or high? And more important, is it in line with the requirements of the situation you are in? Is there anything you should do to change it?

Step 3. Review the power maps of the team members and see if there are matches or mismatches between their deep aspirations and their job requirements.

Questions

Is there anything you can do to redesign jobs so that they fit better with people's expectations? What about job rotation? Some special assignments for particular people?

All we can do is to search for the falsity content of our best theory.

Karl Popper

Part II

Tests and self-assessment exercises

1. My tolerance of ambiguity

A self-assessment exercise on the PTL ambiguity

PART 1

First, reflect on yourself, where you think you are with your life and where you are going to:

1. I think my life is well balanced for the following reasons...
2. I think I am at a crossroads in my life for the following reasons...
3. I think I am in trouble with my life for the following reasons...

PART 2

Now answer the ten questions below (using the proposed scale and any number between 1 and 10):

Scale: 1 (not at all)... 5 (more or less)... 10 (absolutely true)

1. I am quite frustrated with what's happening to me right now
2. I feel uneasy with the direction my life is taking
3. I am tense
4. I experience some kind of uncertainty
5. I am lost
6. I don't know what to do
7. I feel troubled by many things
8. I am surrounded by contradictions
9. I have a sense of loneliness
10. I feel like questioning my core values.

Debriefing

For a score between 10 and 40: There is a good chance that your PTL is stabilised and that you feel quite all right with what's happening to you right now. Your Power-to-Live is well balanced and effectively used, or... are you getting complacent with your life?

For a score between 40 and 80: Yes, you are raising some questions and your Power-to-Live is in the process of being redefined. You are presumably challenging yourself or you have been challenged by your close environment. This could be an opportunity for growth.

For a score between 80 and 100: It seems that you are in a turmoil situation. You may be in pain and reconsidering some critical aspects of your Project-to-Live. It is not an easy phase and certainly not a comfortable situation!

PART 3

Go deeper now and answer the ten following questions (four questionnaires) using the same scale as above.

My main reactions towards what I am experiencing (uncertainty) with my life are basically to:

First questionnaire

1. Ignore what's happening
2. Concentrate on the good aspects of my life
3. Think about something else
4. Invest my time and energy in something that I feel comfortable with
5. Get out of the situation (keep my mind busy)
6. Dream and fantasise about something better
7. Prepare myself for a better time
8. Reflect on my successful past
9. Try to put things into perspective
10. Compare myself to others.

Debriefing

For a score between 10 and 40: You are not withdrawing from the situation and the challenge that you are facing. There is a good chance that you are using another strategy (behaviour) to cope with your 'problems'.

For a score between 40 and 80: You are putting some distance between yourself and what's happening to you. There's nothing wrong with this approach as long as it gives you the proper perspective to act and move on.

For a score between 80 and 100: You are stuck in non-productive behaviour, i.e. the tendency to ignore the issues altogether and flee from the tense situation you are experiencing right now. Is that so?

Second questionnaire

1. Challenge what's occurring
2. Push
3. Get out of it as fast as possible
4. Move ahead
5. Face the situation
6. Stand up and attack
7. Confront the challenges
8. Be aggressive
9. Do something
10. Find a quick way out.

Debriefing

For a score between 10 and 40: Being assertive is not your way. There is a good chance that your approach towards uncertainty and ambiguity is more to stop, take stock, try to understand before acting. You are maybe a bit slow in your reactions... too slow?

For a score between 40 and 80: You are not afraid of standing up and using your energy to fight adversity. There is a good chance that, in a way, you enjoy the challenge of life. You are ready to turn ambiguity into something good for you.

For a score between 80 and 100: Push and win is apparently your way out of a difficult situation. You are a 'fighter'. You may also be perceived by the people around you as somebody who is aggressive, too strong, exhausting and not very deep (maybe you act before thinking?).

Third questionnaire

1. Reflect
2. Try to understand what's happening
3. Take stock
4. Analyse
5. Plan before going ahead
6. Identify the positive and negative aspects of the situation
7. Come up with a change strategy
8. Set up measurements so that I know how well I am doing
9. Come up with alternatives
10. Am very factual.

Debriefing

For a score between 10 and 40: You are not the analytical type. There is a possibility that your actions are based more on your intuition than on a thorough analysis of what's happening to you.

For a score between 40 and 80: You like to understand before doing anything. You enjoy being on top of things. You are reliable and you know what you are talking about. Control (or manage) is the name of the game.

For a score between 80 and 100: You are perhaps lost in too much analysis (*analysis, paralysis*). You over-study and eventually procrastinate. Your decisions may be out of tune with the requirements of the situation that you are in. Too late!

Fourth questionnaire

1. Enjoy being lost
2. See opportunities in ambiguous situations
3. Am not afraid of chaos
4. Question stability anyway
5. Use my imagination to get out of the uncertainty
6. Try various ways to move on
7. Invent and create

8. Borrow from others and build on their ideas

9. Enjoy coming up with new ideas

10. Turn problems into progress and development.

Debriefing

For a score between 10 and 40: You do not feel very comfortable with chaos and uncertainty, do you? You prefer to perform and function in a balanced environment. Are you too conventional and... rigid?

For a score between 40 and 80: You like to explore new ways and behaviour. You use your imagination to turn challenges into personal opportunities. You are creative with your own life. You enjoy the mind expansion process and are not afraid of taking personal risks.

For a score between 80 and 100: You are more on the artistic side of life. You presumably see things that others do not see. You could eventually go overboard with your imagination and jeopardise your own stability (life?). There is also a possibility that others perceive you as being a bit 'crazy'.

PART 4: THE MODEL

Facing personal ambiguity (and we all do from time to time) with our PTL, we have basically four different ways (four questionnaires) of coping:

- Questionnaire 1 is about putting things into perspective.

  It is the ability that we human beings have to take stock of any given situation, look at it from a distance, integrate it into a bigger picture and learn from it before deciding on our next move with our life. Thanks to this natural gift, our PTL is not isolated and locked into a box. It's open to the world. It is alive.

- Questionnaire 2 is about fighting and being assertive.

  The capacity that we have to stand up for what we believe strongly in (our PTL) is also part of our deep identity. We can indeed face adversity, defend ourselves against others' demands and manage conflicts in a positive way. Without the fighting spirit our PTL would remain static. It would not evolve. It would shrink and atrophy.

- Questionnaire 3 is about analysing and understanding.

  Nothing can be done effectively without a minimum of understanding of what's happening and why. The human brain has that capability. We can probe, question, test, experiment, organise, plan and measure. These aptitudes are also critical for our PTLs. Understanding ourselves from a PTL perspective is vital for our sanity and our development.

- Questionnaire 4 is about inventing and innovating.

  This skill is more based on intuition than on rational thinking. It is important to expand our PTL through the identification of new options (invention) and to try them out (innovation). It is the human imagination at work. Our Power-to-Live is mainly dependent on imagination, i.e. on our capacity to enlarge our repertoire of instruments for life.

2. My energy levels or vitality

Instructions

Please select the item you feel more strongly about in each pair. Just circle the appropriate number.

1	I create my own pressure	2	What I enjoy most is to be at peace with myself
3	I value what I have	4	I always look for new opportunities
5	I am often concerned and preoccupied	6	Time solves most problems
7	One of my greatest pleasures comes from achieving	8	Patience is a key to success
9	I get annoyed with pushy people	10	I enjoy working very much
11	To enjoy a meaningful life is one of my top priorities	12	I am always pushing myself further
13	I challenge what's taken for granted (assumptions)	14	Accepting myself is important for me
15	I agree that there are things which can wait until tomorrow	16	I see my life as a constant challenge
17	I believe that, by and large, life is not fair	18	I am basically a self-demanding person
19	I often feel that I haven't done enough	20	I rarely feel guilty
21	I like to move fast with my projects	22	Overall, I am satisfied with what I am and do

II.2. My energy levels or vitality

23	To live and let live is a good motto	24	I believe that life is a struggle
25	I could easily feel bored	26	To be centred and quiet is very important
27	To let go is a sign of intelligence	28	I can be very tenacious
29	I like to make things happen	30	I am convinced that fundamentally life can't be changed
31	When on vacation I like to relax and enjoy myself	32	On holiday I can't help doing things
33	I always want more out of life	34	I am irritated by people who are never satisfied
35	I enjoy the company of people who appreciate life	36	I am attracted to intensely alive people
37	I dream about options and alternatives all the time	38	I believe that we are not always free to decide
39	I enjoy growing and becoming	40	I enjoy being and getting in touch with myself
41	I value what's new	42	I respect the lessons of the past
43	I am convinced that the world will never change	44	I need to be part of what's going on in the world
45	I prefer work to entertainment	46	I believe that working should be fun
47	I believe that sometimes it's better to refrain from acting	48	I often feel impatient
49	People should learn to love each other more	50	The world would be a better place if people would learn how to work together more effectively

Scoring

INSTRUCTIONS

For each of the two following attitudes, please circle the numbers that you have selected. Add up the circles to get two totals:

Attitude A: 1 – 4 – 5 – 7 – 10 – 12 – 13 – 15 – 18 – 19 – 21 – 24 – 25 – 27 – 29 – 32 – 33 – 36 – 37 – 39 – 41 – 44 – 45 – 48 – 50

Total score for Attitude A: _____

Attitude B: 2 – 3 – 6 – 8 – 9 – 11 – 14 – 16 – 17 – 20 – 22 – 23 – 26 – 28 – 30 – 31 – 34 – 35 – 38 – 40 – 42 – 43 – 46 – 47 – 49

Total score for Attitude B: _____

Interpretation

Your Vitality Quotient (VQ) is the degree to which you tend to mobilise/stress your vital functions (your Power-to-Live) in order to ensure the accomplishment of your Project-to-Live. Your VQ measures the intensity of your Will-to-Live.

1. If your score in Attitude B is higher that your score in Attitude A by 15 or more points, your VQ profile is: WITHDRAWN.

Your Will-to-Live is weak or held back. You are not happy with the world or with your life as it is, but you are not disposed to try to change this. You feel generally threatened, both by events and by people. You prefer to disengage yourself than to expose yourself. You want to live a quiet life, far from the turbulence of the world. You have neither strong desires, nor strong ambitions.

By other people, you might be perceived as passive or immobile; as lacking initiative, as not being much of a doer; as someone who prefers contemplation to action.

Your motto is likely to be: 'Don't push the river, it flows anyway.'

2. If your score in Attitude B is higher than your score in Attitude A by between 1 and 14 points, your VQ profile is: CAUTIOUS.

Your Will-to-Live is on standby. You are alert, watching the world around you and evaluating the potential impact of events on your life. You are prepared to react if needed, but you are not disposed to go out and take initiative if not pushed to do so. You will try to avoid risks and to protect yourself against the unexpected. You are reliable as a professional and as a friend, as long as you are not put in a controversial or risky situation. You will go with the general trend of thinking, which you will find reasonable. You like people as a principle, but you will want to check that they are trustworthy. When you feel comfortable with someone, however, you will go out of your way to be helpful.

By others, you might be perceived as a follower rather than as a self-starter; as someone who tends to sit on the fence to see in which direction the wind blows; as trite in your thinking, and not very stimulating.

Your motto is likely to be: 'I prefer to stay on the safe side.'

3. If your score in Attitude A is higher than your score in Attitude B by between 1 and 14 points, your VQ profile is: ENGAGED.

Your Will-to-Live is activated. You are a 'doer'. You can feel the stimulation of the world. Life is full of opportunities which it is fun and useful to exploit. You want to move on: to do things and also to enjoy life. You will take initiative to start new projects, both in your professional and in your personal life. You will be attracted to people that you feel you can do things with – partners more than companions or fellow souls. You like to take responsibility and are not afraid to expose yourself and take risks. You are imaginative in your thinking.

By other people, you are likely to be perceived as a leader, someone with ideas and initiative, active and reliable, interesting. You might also be perceived as overly busy, not available for pleasure or relaxation, not really interested in other people's personal feelings or problems, self-centred.

Your motto is likely to be: 'Let's do it!'

4. If your score in Attitude A is higher than your score in Attitude B by 15 or more points, you VQ Profile is: HYPERACTIVE.

Your Will-to-Live is overwhelming. You are an 'entrepreneur', a 'conqueror'. You feel the pressure inside you constantly. You can never really relax, and when you have fun or indulge in entertainment, you are always still thinking of some work that you need to do. You need to be engaged in a project and to feel that you are constantly expanding your Power-to-Live. For you, 'the world is up for grabs'! You are impatient, never satisfied, except for short moments of achievement. You need to lead, to take charge, lest things not move fast or effectively enough, or go 'your way'. Other people are essentially vectors of your own enterprises; you need them to carry forward your projects. You are not really interested in their personal lives. You are very creative. You are of the stuff that can make great leaders, provided you don't overdo it...

By others, you are likely to be perceived as hyperactive, very imaginative, always on the go, innovative. On a less positive side, you could also be perceived as too pushy, arrogant, aggressive, tiring and bossy; as a never satisfied workaholic, who does not understand the real values of life; as insensitive to other people and inadequate in carrying out your personal life.

Your motto is likely to be: 'More is better.'

3. My emotional quotient

Assessment questionnaire

INSTRUCTIONS

Please select *one* item per line, the one that you feel most accurately describes you now. Circle the number that corresponds to the item you have selected.

1. I do not feel happy	2. I feel like reflecting on life	3. I like myself very much
4. I am proud of the way my life is running	5. I'd rather be with other people than alone	6. I feel frustrated
7. I am trying to find my way	8. Something important is missing	9. I feel that I am growing/expanding
10. It can be nice/useful to be with other people	11. I am at a waiting stage	12. Sometimes I wonder if it's all really worth the effort
13. Most of the time I perceive other people as a threat	14. I am prudent and cautious	15. I see life as a great challenge and I love it
16. I think that life is enjoyable	17. I am always concerned about what's ahead	18. I feel dejected
19. I withdraw	20. I can't find the time to do everything that I want to do	21. I don't feel sufficiently challenged
22. I know that I should do better	23. My talents are fully used	24. I feel depressed
25. I need support and help	26. I don't like taking risks	27. I trust myself

28. I feel like a winner	29. *Que sera sera* (What will be, will be)	30. I worry a lot

SCORING

Please circle below all the numbers you have selected.

State 1: 1 – 6 – 8 – 12 – 13 – 18 – 19 – 24 – 25 – 30
Give yourself **1** point for each selected number.
Total: _____

State 2: 2 – 5 – 7 – 11 – 14 – 17 – 21 – 22 – 26 – 29
Give yourself **3** points for each selected number.
Total: _____

State 3: 3 – 4 – 9 – 10 – 15 – 16 – 20 – 23 – 27 – 28
Give yourself **5** points for each selected number.
Total: _____

Grand Total: _____

INTERPRETATION

The Emotional Quotient (EQ) reflects your own overall evaluation, at a given moment in time, of the state of your Project-to-Live and of its chances of accomplishment. Your EQ, as such, will directly affect the judgement you pass on and the value you give to any person, object or event that you then encounter in the course of your existence.

1. For a score between 10 and 25:

It could be that your Project-to-Live is in trouble. Something is not right. Your vital functions are strangled. You feel stymied. You are struggling to find a way out. You feel vulnerable and lost.

Better to do something to re-align your Project-to-Live. Have a good look at your private and professional lives. Maybe you need help. Make a diagnosis of what's wrong. Find a way to change and stop shrinking!

2. For a score between 25 and 40:

You are OK. Your Project-to-Live is basically on the right track. This does not mean you are totally comfortable or carefree.

There is a good chance that you feel you could do better or more. Maybe you are over-prudent. It's perhaps time to build on some of your talents (check your Power-to-Live!), to take risks, to activate new vital functions. Maybe you need to wake up and energise yourself!

3. For a score between 40 and 50:

Your Project-to-Live is fully activated and running. You feel in good shape and that you are what you are 'supposed' to be. You are fulfilling your top expectations. You are expanding. But be careful: this could be overwhelming and maybe even blinding. Keep an eye on 'inflation'. Go for it and... keep checking your emotions!

4. My courage

Self-assessment on risk taking and courage

The leader is a role model. People are looking up at their leaders and learning from them. The issue is: How good are you as a leader at taking charge, owning, being responsible for what you say and do?

Are you in charge?

Please assess yourself on the scale below. Be as candid as possible.

1 (Not at all)... 3 (Moderately so)... 5 (Very much so)

How good are you at:

1. Standing up for your own ideas
2. Speaking up in front of intimidating people
3. Being a champion and putting your career on the line
4. Fighting for new ideas
5. Going against the trend
6. Facing conflicts and confrontations
7. Questioning somebody's authority
8. Defending other people when they are in trouble
9. Challenging the norm
10. Showing your weaknesses
11. Owning your ideas when there is a risk
12. Coping with adversity
13. Volunteering for risky actions
14. Making decisions when in doubt
15. Not giving up easily

16. Exploring new ways and avenues
17. Controlling your fear
18. Saying no
19. Not panicking easily
20. Enjoying tension
21. Smiling when in trouble
22. Daring when things are not clear
23. Taking risks when afraid
24. Having guts and being bold
25. Deciding without being sure
26. Taking responsibility
27. Stretching myself by challenging my own habits
28. Being unconventional
29. Letting go and trusting people
30. Admitting that you do not know something.

DEBRIEFING

For a score between 30 and 80: There is a possibility that you are an overcautious leader. You play it safe (too safe?). You reflect before acting and take your time when deciding. You are not inclined to take risks (only calculated risks). You do not enjoy the unknown. You are careful (shy?). You are not very fond of quick, unexpected change and are maybe afraid of 'rocking the boat'!

For a score between 80 and 120: There is a possibility that you are ready to take risk and that you actually do it. You are not afraid of failing. You can be bold at times without being 'crazy'. You enjoy trying new things. You stand up and fight for your ideas. You believe in 'no pain, no gain', and you keep asking questions, probing, exploring and discovering. You are a challenger and love to 'shake the coconut tree'!

For a score between 120 and 150: There is a possibility that you are over-courageous. You decide quickly (too quickly?) and your decisions are more based on inspiration and intuition than on reflection and understanding. You can be defined as unreliable. You ignore the potential danger of the situation that you are in. You go ahead without thinking. You can be wild (foolish?) at times, and be perceived by the people around you as being 'a loose cannon'.

5. My art of living

Checking on your personal 'art of living'

Have a good look at your personal life and your repertoire of ready-made answers. How do you usually react when you:

1. Work

   How do you handle your job? How do you work with other people? How do you relate to your boss?

2. Spend money

   How do you value money? On what do you spend it? How much do you spare? Are you generous? Do you talk openly about it?

3. Are in love

   How do you express your feelings? How do you talk to the other person? Do you behave in a romantic way? Are you gentle and nice? Are you provocative and challenging?

4. Must change

   How do you define change? Do you enjoy it? Do you like to move fast? Do you prefer to control things and go step by step?

5. Relax

   How do you rest and relax? Do you practise any sport? Which one(s)? When? Do you manage your spare time in a systematic way? How do you organise your vacation?

6. Learn

   How do you look at your own development? Do you read a lot? Are you interested in art? What kind? What do you do (attend concerts, go to exhibitions...)?

7. Raise children

How do you go about educating your children? How do you motivate them to grow and acquire proper values and behaviour? Do you talk to them? Do you care?

8. Eat

How do you look at food? Do you enjoy eating? When? What? When? Where?

9. Sleep

Do you enjoy sleeping? Is it important for you? How much time do you devote to sleeping? Do you dream a lot? Do you share your dreams with others?

10. Take care of domestic tasks

Do you like to take care of maintenance activities? Do you clean things around you? Do you care about appearance? Do you like order?

6. My creative leadership profile

Are you a creative leader? We suggest that you, the reader, go through the following self-assessment exercise first before reading further. In other words, look at where you are strong and maybe not so strong in relation to leading in a creative way.

Assess yourself on the following scale:

- That's not me at all (between 1 and 3)

- Yes, I do this at least from time to time (between 3 and 7)

- It is absolutely typical of me. I do this all the time (between 7 and 10).

Observation: We advise you to give yourself a 1 if you do not understand the item!

How good are you at:

1. Challenging your basic ways of being
2. Trusting your insights even when they are disturbing
3. Behaving with flexibility
4. Enjoying people's ability to challenge you with new ideas
5. Creating a mind-expansion environment within your team
6. Putting creativity first in your corporate value system
7. Revisiting the concept of leadership from time to time
8. Trying new leadership behaviours
9. Learning from leadership trials and errors
10. Feeling good about the unexpected
11. Improving your leadership behaviour systematically
12. Encouraging people to discover their own inventiveness

13. Leading your team with imagination
14. Playing the organisational power game in a smart way
15. Integrating various leadership models
16. Testing unconventional leadership skills
17. Sharing your leadership learning with others
18. Knowing why you know what you know
19. Turning your mistakes into opportunities
20. Making sure that people around you come up with new ideas
21. Leading 'stars' and 'solid performers' with imagination
22. Creating a corporate structure conductive to innovation
23. Inventing your own leadership way
24. Assessing your leadership creativity systematically
25. Keeping a leadership diary
26. Not taking anything about yourself for granted
27. Not being afraid of loving
28. Acknowledging that each individual is a gold mine
29. Making sure that the team outperforms the team members through synergy
30. Viewing problems as opportunities
31. Getting leadership inspirations from other cultures
32. Adapting your leadership behaviours to new conditions
33. Learning how to learn about leadership
34. Inventing new assumptions about yourself
35. Exploring new feelings
36. Surprising your team with new ways of working together
37. Acting as a champion of new ideas in your organisation
38. Imagining new approaches to leadership
39. Experimenting with new leadership models
40. Contributing to the enhancement of leadership theories
41. Experimenting with new patterns of thinking

42. Being excited about becoming different

43. Questioning the relevance of your own behaviour in some situations

44. Triggering passion for innovation in others

45. Surprising yourself with spontaneous moves.

ASSESSING YOUR CREATIVE LEADERSHIP STRENGTHS

First look at your overall score:

The shadow creative leader

If your grand total is between 45 and 100: Well, let's face it, creative leadership is not your cup of tea. There are perhaps quite a few good explanations for that low score on creative leadership. Either:

- It is not part of your psychological profile and never will be. Nothing wrong with that; it won't prevent you living a good and successful life.

- There is no need for you to be creative because the job that you have does not require it.

- You are – on the contrary – extremely creative, and this is why you did not believe in the exercise and went through it 'playing' with the questions in a kind of loose way.

The shy creative leader

If your grand total score is between 100 and 250: You have the potential to be creative but it is perhaps quite possible that you do not activate your creative leadership skills as often as you could (should?). It may be that you are missing a few opportunities:

- To outperform yourself by tapping into your creative leadership mind.

- To give a chance to the people who are working with you to be more and better.

- To contribute to the success of your organisation in a more effective way.

The performing creative leader

If your grand total score is between 250 and 350: It seems that not only do you know what creative leadership is all about but that you are also:

- Enjoying acting as a creative leader. You are at ease with reinventing yourself and growing from your own drive to become what you are deep down inside.

- Challenging your team and team members in a very innovative way. There is a good chance that you are the kind of leader who is able to manage what we call a mind-expansion environment for the people who are working with you.

- Being a source of new ideas, projects and actions in your organisation. You are never short of ideas about what could happen as well as about the future of the company that you belong to. Be careful though as this could be a source of heavy frustration if the corporate environment does not give you a fair chance to carry out your 'brilliant' suggestions.

The overboard creative leader

If your grand total score is between 350 and 450: There is no question that this is too high and could create major problems for you, your team members and your organisation, for instance:

- You are so creative that you lost your own sense of identity. Too many directions, too many options, too much creativity can be a source of major disruptions in your life.

- The people in your team find you unpredictable and difficult to read. They do not know how to approach you, and on top of that, they never know if you are serious about some of your ideas or not. There is a strong possibility that you have lost your credibility.

- The top managers of your organisation are concerned about you and your behaviour. They do not think that you are reliable or that you should be trusted because you are so far away from the norms... This has happened to many geniuses in the past...

Let's now go deeper and have a good look at the three critical dimensions of creative leadership, i.e.

- Leading yourself
- Leading others
- Leading the field.

LEADING YOURSELF ('LY')

Creative thinking (items 1 – 18 – 26 – 34 – 41)

If your total score on the items on pages 232 to 234 is between 15 and 50: There is a good chance that your way of thinking is close to being traditional, conservative and linear.

If your total score is between 50 and 100: You can – if needed and asked to – think in a non-linear way.

If your total score is between 100 and 150: This is what we call 'lateral thinking' (de Bono). It is based on the use of alternatives to the 'cause and effect' way of understanding things, i.e. unconventional associations, synchronicity.

Creative feeling (items 2 – 10 – 27 – 35 – 42)

If your total score on the items is between 15 and 50: Feelings are not perceived by you as a good source of inspiration. Maybe you should challenge your assumptions.

If your total score is between 50 and 100: You are not afraid of listening to your feelings and follow what they tell you.

If your total score is between 100 and 150: You are for certain emotionally creative... too much maybe?

Creative behaving (items 3 – 11 – 19 – 43 – 45)

If your total score on the above items is between 15 and 50: Your behaviour is not characterised by a high degree of creativity. Maybe you do not need it.

If your total score is between 50 and 100: You are not afraid of trying new ways to act and perform. You are open to trial and error and learn from the process.

If your total score is between 100 and 150: Your motto is 'If it is new and different it must be good.' You are at the forefront of the new wave, and you are indeed highly creative not just in word but also in deeds.

LEADING OTHERS ('LO')

Leading individuals (items 4 – 12 – 20 – 28 – 44)

If your total score on the items is between 15 and 50: You are not that interested in other people and in their development. Your basic way to lead others is to tell them what you expect and they just deliver. No fuss, no muss.

If your total score is between 50 and 100: You care about other individuals and you are ready to invest time and energy in their development. You relate to individuals with flexibility and a touch of creativity. You believe that each individual has some unique potential and that it is up to you – as a leader – to help them grow and expand.

If your total score is between 100 and 150: You are overdoing it. Your main centre of interest is the individuals who are working with you. You will try everything to wake them up and get them moving.

Leading teams (items 5 – 13 – 21 – 29 – 36)

If your total score on the items is between 15 and 50: No need to elaborate; you do not believe in teamwork.

If your total score is between 50 and 100: You are convinced that by putting individual brains together you are able to create a big plus or a major added value. It is called 'synergy', and you believe in it.

If your total score is between 100 and 150: You are addicted to teamwork and apt to forget that teams also exist to deliver outstanding results and not just to satisfy people's social needs. You are creative, but not necessarily in the 'right' direction.

Leading organisations (items 6 – 14 – 22 – 30 – 37)

If your total score on the above items is between 15 and 50: You manage organisations in a standard (and presumably effective) way. There's not much imagination in the way you lead your business unit or corporation. Is this good enough?

If your total score is between 50 and 100: You do manage your organisation with a bit of innovation and risk taking. You are not afraid of involving the members of the organisations in the reinvention of your company.

If your total score is between 100 and 150: You are hopefully leading a start-up or a brand new high-tech company. You thrive on creativity. It is your life.

LEADING THE FIELD ('LF')

Creating concepts (items 7 – 15 – 23 – 31 – 38)

If your total score on the items is between 15 and 50: You are not that interested in exploring the basic assumptions that underline leadership. You leave that kind of research to the scholars and the academics.

If your total score is between 50 and 100: You enjoy being an active partner in the creation of the new leadership concepts. You read about leadership. You contribute to the advancement of the field.

If your total score is between 100 and 150: I hope you are in an academic position because you are obviously deeply interested in leadership research; or perhaps a consultant who is not afraid of presenting new leadership ideas to your clients.

Creating practices (items 8 – 16 – 24 – 32 – 39)

If your total score on the items is between 15 and 50: You listen to those who know something about leadership and follow their advice. You behave according to the established leadership models.

If your score is between 50 and 100: You like to try out new leadership behaviours on your own. You produce your own ideas on how a leader should behave; you try them out and then share the result with other people.

If your score is between 100 and 150: Your main concern as a leader is to experiment with new ways of leading, learn something from your own experience and spread the 'good word' around you.

Creating the field (items 9 – 17 – 25 – 33 – 40)

If your total score on the items is between 15 and 50: You are more a user of leadership concepts and models than a source of innovation in the field.

If your total score is between 50 and 100: You like to think that you are participating in the advancement of the leadership field by your work, reflection and learning.

If your total score is between 100 and 150: You perceive yourself as a good contributor to the reinvention of the leadership theories. You keep track of your own discoveries in a systematic way and you are not afraid of writing about and publishing them.

7. My power quotient

This exercise is about measuring to what extent you are clear about your life aspirations and able to satisfy them, and the effect this match or mismatch is having on your VQ.

Instructions

Please assess yourself by applying to the following statements a scale from 1 to 10, according to how much they reflect the way you think about yourself. Any number between 1 and 10 can be applied.

- I'm quite sure of my life priorities...
- I do have some particularly strong aspirations...
- I'm quite stable in my interests in life...
- I'm currently fully dedicated to one strong interest ...
- I don't spend too much time on introspection and soul-searching...
- There is nothing really blocking my way ...
- There are no obligations preventing me from doing what I really want to do...
- I am a good self-starter...
- I'm getting all the support I need to really get to do things the way I'd like to...
- I know I can do more and I know just how...
- Everything is going my way ...
- For me the glass is more often half full than half empty...
- I don't have to settle for compromises in my life...
- I expect to get from life as much as it can give me...
- I don't feel held back ...

- I feel that I'm really getting somewhere...
- I'm living at my full capacity...
- I don't feel frustrated...
- I think my life is evolving the right way...
- I have a lot of opportunities in front of me ...
- I lead my life...
- I enjoy my work fully...
- I really believe that I have everything I need to run my life the way I want it...
- I know what I want...
- My life objectives are crystal clear...
- I think I am on the right track with my life...
- Life is treating me well...
- I am full of resources...
- I am in a position to decide on my life objectives...
- I would not change anything in my life...

Total: _____

Debriefing

1. Reduce your total score by 50 points
2. Interpretation:

    A: From 0 to 50: *You don't really know what you want*

    You are not focused on any real priority. You are attracted by everything and nothing. You try one thing and move on to something else. You don't feel that your life has any particular meaning or purpose. You often wish you could get fully engaged in one driving interest that would really mobilise your attention and energy. You probably need to work on your Power Map and get to understand it better, so that your real life priorities can appear to you more clearly.

The higher your potential VQ, the more the chances are of a VQ gap, which makes you feel frustrated and impatient, and blocked in your need for expansion.

B: From 50 to 100: *You know what you want but you're stuck*

You have a driving aim, a need to accomplish, achieve, complete something in particular, but there are obstacles, roadblocks that keep you from getting there. Or maybe you don't know where or how to get started. You feel frustrated and held back. You need to examine whether these obstacles are external or coming from within you (they could be excuses that you are giving yourself for not finding the way or energy to get started). If they are indeed external, then your priority is to clear the way or get around the roadblocks. Check your Power Map again: maybe it's not what you thought, and that may explain why you're stuck.

Anyway, don't just sit there and brood!

The higher your potential VQ, the more your VQ gap is yawning because of this stalled situation and the more your vitality is pressing for you to get unstuck and take off.

C: From 100 to 200: *You are getting more or less what you want*

You are feeling pretty good with your life. Your priorities are fairly clear and nothing really is getting in the way of your accomplishing what you want to do.

Sure, everything is not perfect: sometimes you set a course and you find out that you're running up a dead end, but then you are able to readjust. You also often run against obstacles, but that's life, isn't it? It's even fun to overcome such roadblocks! However, let's be honest: there are times when you wonder whether you are really on the right track or whether you should be re-orientating yourself to something more meaningful, more in line with what you are really expecting from life. You've probably got a good reading of your Power Map overall, but if what was just mentioned is happening, have another look!

There is a good chance that your VQ gap is narrow and that you are feeling good overall, but if your vitality is very strong you could be craving for even more!

D: From 200 to 250: *You are fully empowered with your life*

Life is great, isn't it? Things are really going your way. Not only do you know what you want, but you are in a situation where nothing prevents you from getting there. You found a perfect match between your deep life aspirations (your Power Map) and the occupation that matches them. You can get exactly as much as you are willing to put in. Sure it's hard, exacting, and you have to give up on other things, like your personal life at times perhaps; but overall you know that's the price to pay in order to achieve the greater purpose of your life. No reason for you not to keep it up as long as you feel good about it. Be careful however about shifting the cost of it all to the people close to you: it could end up hurting more than you are aware of today...

Your VQ gap is as narrowed down as can reasonably be expected and therefore you feel that you are living a fulfilling life, even though your very strong vitality quotient may never feel completely satisfied!

3. Finally, discuss the three highest and the three lowest scores with the person next to you.

Part III
The PTL journal

Introduction

This is a journal. It is intended to be your 'PTL journal'. The idea is to use a journal (diary) to keep track of some of your life events, record your thoughts and feelings at the time of their occurrence, analyse them according to the PTL model and finally help you decide on the best course of action so that you can indeed have 'a better life'.

As you can see, there are six parts in the journal. You can use them in the following ways:

1. You start with section 1 and move along at your own pace. It is easy and can be very effective because of the rationale behind the model.

2. You pick the section which appeals most to you right now, and then proceed according to your needs and expectations. You use the prototype journal in a flexible way so that you focus on what is important for you right now.

3. You just look at the end of each day at what happened to you and then use the appropriate section to register your behaviours, thoughts and emotions, as well as what you have learned from them. In other words, you create your own philosophical (PTL) journal.

However, it seems that the journal will be particularly powerful if you follow the following guidelines:

- Use the journal on a daily basis. Never skip a day. Be consistent and regular.

- Be thorough and do not hesitate to go back to the model when going through the analysis part.

- Do stop at the end of four weeks or after a major life or professional event to reflect on what happened and learn as much as possible from it.

Again, what you have below is just a sample of what you can do. It is up to you to decide on how you want to look at yourself. Keep in mind that by deciding you own your life!

1. My key questions about life in general

Part 1. Identification

At this point in time in my life, I am really concerned with:

Part 2. Daily events

Today, the following events occurred and had an impact on me:

- What happened is:
- My behaviour:
- My emotions:
- My thoughts:

Part 3. The analysis

Looking at my behaviour, emotions and thoughts and using the PTL model, I learned:

Part 4. Decision for action

I really believe that I could enhance the quality of my life by (doing what and how):

- Action 1
- Action 2
- Action 3

Part 5. Debriefing

Revisiting what I wrote some time ago, I now feel that:

- I have learnt the following about myself:

- I have improved in the following areas:
- I could still improve by doing the following:

Checkpoint

Identify a person whom you trust and who knows you quite well. Now ask that person to think about you and write down his or her answers to the following question:

I perceive M— as being a person who... (Please write one page in an open and free way):

Look at the written page and compare with what you wrote before. Get at least three insights out of the comparison:

1.

2.

3.

If you feel comfortable enough with the person chosen you can maybe have a good (verbal) exchange of impressions about what you wrote about yourself, and what he or she said about you. Your choice...!

2. My philosophical intentions

Let's look at the future and see what kind of orientations your life could take for the better! We shall go step by step and cover:

- Tomorrow
- One month from now
- One year from now
- My life in general
- Checkpoint

Tomorrow

Identify (today) three things you would like to try out, test or verify during your day tomorrow:

- First, about you (i.e. is it really true that...?):
- Second, about you in relation with others (i.e. I must ask people if I really...?):
- Third, about you and your environment (i.e. I must check what my 'boss', my colleagues, team members think about me?):

Write down (at the end of the day) your answers to the three selected questions:

1.

2.

3.

Stop now and reflect on what the answers are telling you about:

- The way you perceive or define yourself:
- The way other people look at you and see you:
- The way you relate to a system (organisation):

One month from now

On the basis of the one-day exercise, decide on what you would like to achieve in a one-month period starting tomorrow. More specifically, make up your mind about the following:

- Three things you want to do more because you like it and it is good for you:

- Three things you want to stop doing because you do not think that it is right for you:

- Three things you would like to do differently because it would serve you better:

At the end of the month check your success or failure and decide what to do next!

One year from now

Let's now go for the real and deep issues. The idea is for you to sit down in a very quiet environment and, without any interruption, write down your answer to the following question:

- If everything was possible, I would love to (be what, do what, change what)... Write three pages on your dreams about yourself.

Looking back at what you wrote, single out three elements that you think are absolutely critical for you and go through the following analysis:

- What do they mean for you and how important are they and why?

- What prevents you from being it or doing it?

- What can you do to change the present situation and get there?

My life in general

Please complete the following sentence: *I strongly believe that to be happier, I must...*

Stop now and think about the philosophical implications of what you just wrote.

- What does it mean for you?

- How important is it?

- What can you do to make it happen?

Checkpoint

Identify a person (someone new) who knows you and whom you trust, and ask him or her to answer (one page in writing) the following question: *I believe that M— would be much happier if... (what?)*

3. My Will-to-Live

You are now ready to use the PTL model in a more straightforward way. Let us start with the Will-to-Live and examine it from three different perspectives:

- The fundamentals
- The daily dimension
- The social aspects

The fundamentals

Isolate yourself and write down your answers to the three following questions:

- Question 1. How do you assess the quality of your basic drive at this point in time in your life? (We suggest that you revisit the fourth chapter of the book as well as the test on the VQ while answering.)

- Question 2. Is the Will-to-Live your fundamental reference? If not, what is it and what are the implications for your own life?

- Question 3. Do you feel the desire to live in you? How does it express itself?

The daily dimension

Pick up a day of your life (you can repeat this process as many times as you wish), look back at what happened during the day and put down your thoughts about:

- How did the basic drive (the Will-to-Live) express itself during your day?

- Check on the emotions (see Chapter 7 as well as the test on the EQ) that you experienced during the day and identify what they are telling you about your Project-to-Live:

- From your daily experience, identify what you could do to enhance the success of your PTL (don't be afraid of being selfish):

The social aspects

Please look back again at your day and identify three people that you interacted with, and then take some time to reflect on:

- The drive that is behind each person's life
- The basic motivation behind each person's actions
- The self-centred orientation of anybody's behaviour.

Checkpoint

Try to organise a meeting (it might be a very pleasant meal together) with two or three people that you feel comfortable with, and have a two- to three-hour discussion on:

'If the ultimate reference is our Will-to-Live, then we should:'

- Pay attention to... (what? and why?)
- Do (what? and why?)
- Forget about (what? and why?)

The exchange could also focus on: 'We reject the idea of the Will-to-Live because...' If you select this option, then it is important to explore the alternative that you are using as ultimate reference(s) and its consequences.

4. My Power-to-Live

Again, we strongly recommend you to go back to Chapter 5 before starting this part of your journal.

This part is different from what you did before. We suggest that you set up and implement a 180° feedback process. It could go as follows:

Step 1

Review the suggested questionnaire presented below and modify it to make sure that it suits you well (you should feel comfortable with all the questions and their formulations).

Step 2

Go through the questionnaire yourself and answer all the questions as thoroughly as possible (replace your name by 'I').

Step 3

Identify three people who know you quite well and ask them to go through the same questionnaire thinking about you. (Please make sure that they fully understand what it is all about, and that they are as candid as possible when answering. Also try to do it with one person who is a peer or a friend; another who has some kind of 'power' over you; and thirdly someone that you have some 'power' over.

Step 4

Collect the filled-out questionnaire and read all the answers carefully. Compare them with your own answers as well as with each other.

Step 5

Make some entries in your journal to summarise the key lesson from the exercise and the key actions you envisage taking to improve your life.

The Power Map feedback questionnaire

- I believe that M—'s major strengths in life are (please list at least three):
- I believe that M—'s major personal weaknesses are (please list at least three):

Please assess M—'s behaviour using the listing below as well as the following scale (feel free to use any number between 1 and 10):

1 (not at all like him)... 5 (somewhat like him)... 10 (quite like him)

M— enjoys:

- Being left alone
- Creating new things
- Working with other people
- Learning and growing
- Giving and receiving help
- Challenging people
- Bargaining and negotiating
- Probing and asking questions
- Winning
- Caring about himself/herself
- Spending time with his/her family
- Making money
- Being in charge and having power
- Buying new things

- Being the centre of attention
- Friendship
- Reading
- Owning things
- Being spiritual and religious
- Being good at what he/she is doing

Others:

- In which situation(s) do you think that M— is very successful? Why?
- What, according to you, makes M— different from everybody else?
- What would you recommend M— to do in order to have a better life?
- Do you remember a time when M— was very happy? When was it? Why was M— happy?
- A time when he/she was very unhappy? Why?
- Describe where M— could be in five years from now:
- Use one word to summarise your impression of M—:

Summarise here what you have learnt from the feedback exercise:

Checkpoint

Choose from what the people interviewed said about you something that upset you very much and deconstruct it the following way:

STEP 1
Think about why it upsets you so much (your emotions are telling you something about your PTL!).

STEP 2
Arrange a meeting with one of the interviewees (anyone, as long

as you feel comfortable with that person and trust him or her) and challenge that person on the very same idea ('It cannot be true...', 'Give me an example...').

STEP 3

Put a note in your journal about the conclusion you have reached at the end of this exercise (something meaningful for you).

5. My Way-to-Live

Without deeds and actions it is all words! So have a look at the way you implement your PTL. This time we recommend that you take one week at a time, and this over a one-month period:

- Week 1: What is work for you?
- Week 2: How do you handle ethical matters?
- Week 3: Do you own your life?
- Week 4: Where do you stand with your life?

Week 1. What is work for you?

The idea is to concentrate (during the entire week) on three questions:

1. How do you assess the activation of our vital functions during the week?

What you can do is to monitor your week by keeping a diary focusing on: What were my key actions today? What thrilled me during the day? What else could I have done?

- Day 1:
- Day 2:
- Day 3:
- Day 4:
- Day 5:
- Day 6:
- Day 7:

At the end of the week, summarise your learning and your decisions regarding the enhancement of your Way-to-Live.

2.   How do you cope with pleasure and entertainment?

Just list at the beginning, in the middle and at the end of the week the actions taken in order to:

- Relax and rest
- Recharge your batteries
- Avoid boredom
- Intensify your impression of living
- Cope with stress
- Change the pace of your life
- Anything else?

Looking back at the list, can you now identify any patterns and see if this is what you want? (Any boredom?)

Are you really happy with your life?

This is a serious issue. Use the three scales below and then reflect on what's best for you.

This week I have experienced:

- Some deep, negative emotions...
- No special emotions...
- Some great, positive emotions

Think about what those emotions (or the lack of them) are telling you about yourself, the state of your PTL and what should be done to have a better life.

- A very low level of energy...
- A medium level of energy...
- A very high level of energy

What are those levels telling you about yourself and your life? What do you prefer? What can you do to live at the 'right' (for you) energy level?

- Mediocre results...
- No results...
- Great results

257

Look at your actions and measure their effectiveness or success. Have you achieved what you intended to achieve or not? If yes, what do you learn from it? If not, why so? What can you do to become more efficient? Have a good look at your behaviour and see if you really do what you should be doing...

Week 2. How do you handle ethical matters?

This is a special week... and not an easy one! The challenge is for you to determine the matches and mismatches between your own code of conduct and the ones of the various institutions that you interface with. This time you should concentrate on all the conflicts that you experience during the week and see if there is any contradiction between your model and other people's way of living. So the process should go like this:

Step 1: Spot the conflicting situation or event.

Step 2: Look at the ethical (our definition) contradictions that can be the cause of the conflict.

Step 3: Identify the learning from your diagnosis and decide on how to improve your overall situation.

Here are the various situations you should look at:

- You and your family (parents, children, spouse)
- You and your organisation (where you have a job)
- You and your friends
- You and other people in general
- You and the church that you belong to
- You and your hobbies (sports)
- You and your 'service contacts' (bank, garage, doctor etc.)
- Anything else?

Week 3. Do you own your life?

Now you should be ready to tackle the crucial question of ownership. Do you own your life? Are you in charge of your life?

This is what we propose for this very important exercise:

Each evening you prepare a list of things you are going to do the day after to show to yourself that you are indeed in charge of your own life, i.e. the decisions and actions related to:

- your private life
- your professional life
- your leisure life

The key question here is 'How can you show to yourself that you are indeed responsible for your life?'

You review what happened at the end of the day and prepare (proactively) your actions for the following day.

Well, maybe you do not own your life... What does it mean for you then?

CHECKPOINT

Identify somebody whom you feel is fully in charge of his/her life and interview him/her. We suggest that you tape (with his or her permission) the interview so that you can play it back later on. We also submit the following list of questions for you to use at your discretion:

Tentative questions:

- How do you feel about your life in general?
- Do you feel in charge of your life?
- What makes you think that you are in charge?
- What do you do to be in charge?
- Is it important for you (to be in charge)?
- Do you tend to look for scapegoats when you have a problem?
- Do you tend to blame others or 'fate' when bad things happen to you? Conversely, do you tend to thank fate or heaven for the good things that you encounter?

- How do you cope with pressure from outside?
- Do you feel responsible for what happens to you?
- What would you like to change in your life?
- What have your learnt from your past experience?
- Where do you see yourself tomorrow?

Week 4. Where do you stand with your life?

You have to conclude... This is also a very important step in the PTL process. You must look at the big picture and get the essentials out of the first three weeks.

This exercise deserves a special (and demanding exercise). We ask you now to write between ten and twenty pages on yourself. You must put down at least two pages a day on... *you!* In other words, we are asking you to write your own PTL book.

Here is a (purely indicative) example of an outline that you can use:

Introduction: *The person I think I am is...*

- Part 1. If I am the reference, then...
- Part 2. My energy level is...
- Part 3. What drives me right now is...
- Part 4. I manage my life by...
- Part 5. What is important for me is...

Transition: *The person people think I am is...*

- Part 6. My emotions are telling me...
- Part 7. I really could be more...
- Part 8. My main problem with other people is...
- Part 9. My behaviour seems to me...
- Part 10. I need courage to...

Conclusion: *The person I want to be is...*

And now, the process starts again – your way! It never stops as long as we are alive.

6. Becoming a creative leader

This is about how the PTL can help you become a more effective leader. Does the fact that you can now better understand what it is that makes people tick, and what makes them feel what they feel and do what they do, give you new insights on how you can better lead them, so that they can reach higher performance and enjoy more what they do?

Question 1

Do you feel that you now have a better understanding of your business partners' behaviours (team members, boss, partners...)? In what way?

Are you more aware of their vitality quotient?

Do you read deeper into their life aspirations (Power Maps)?

Are you more skilful in interpreting their emotions?

Question 2

What can you do now in the workplace, thanks to your PTL knowledge, to be a stronger leader?

How will you take into account the differences in the VQ of your various business partners?

How will you match Power Maps and work assignments?

How will you acknowledge the messages that your team members' emotions are conveying to you?

Question 3

What will you do about your own self as a leader?

Are you sure your job matches your own VQ?

Are you fulfilling your deeper life needs? What can you do to find a better match?

Are you feeling good? How is your EQ? Is your present position satisfying your PTL, or are there some serious frustrations around? What can you do about it?

Have you thought about the fact that your own lack of fulfil-
ment could negatively impact on your effectiveness as a leader?

Is your PTL at work in a good enough shape that you can be
perceived as a powerful role model?

Try to give your team members a chance to give you some
feedback on:

- you as a leader

- them as they feel in their current assignments

- how they would like to see things change.

Try to translate their feedback comments into 'PTL' language, so
that you can act in relation to VQ, Power Maps, emotions, ethics
etc.

Make notes of all this and check your notes periodically.
What have you done since you last checked? If there are
problems, don't sit on them! They won't go away unless *you*
make them disappear...

Glossary

ambiguity
A situation that presents different possible meanings, none of which is in itself satisfying. Ambiguity leaves us with a feeling of perplexity and uneasiness. Ambiguity is a kind of unsettled knowledge; not understanding exactly where we stand – we don't feel in full control of our PTL. There are ways to deal with ambiguity which enable us to alleviate this negative impression and strengthen our position when confronted with such situations.

art of living
Our art of living is the optimisation of our behaviour, the way by which we have learnt to mobilise our vital functions so as to ensure the best accomplishment of our PTL through the proper usage of our vital functions. Our art of living implies the best possible balance between the output of our actions, the degree to which they mobilise our vital capacities and their cost, in terms of Power-to-Live (see *equation of life*).

behaviour
In our usage, our behaviour is just another word for our Way-to-Live. In this sense we use the word differently from and more broadly than the way that it is understood in behavioural sciences. Our behaviour includes actions, emotions and rest.

beauty
It is the measure by which we value the conformity of a thing (object, person, idea) to our total representation of the world and of our life (our knowledge). A thing is all the more beautiful if it is able to completely

evoke in us our idea of the world and life. A work of art will be deemed beautiful according to its ability to bring to our minds and our sensations the greatest number of aspects of our PTL with the greatest intensity.

boredom   An impression that comes to us as a result of the underutilisation of our vital functions. By leaving them idle, and not devoting them to the implementation of our PTL, we fail to satisfy our Will-to-Live and therefore go against our actual *raison d'être*. As a result, our PTL sends us a negative emotion that we call boredom.

courage   An attitude which reflects our determination to act while risking to harm our Power-to-Live already acquired. The reason we take such risks is that we have calculated that it is to our advantage to do so, so that one can say that we are never actually courageous in our own eyes. It is only others who can see us as courageous, when they watch us and think, *I would never have dared to do that myself!* – meaning that their own evaluation of the pros and cons of the situation would have been different from ours, and that for them the cons would probably have outweighed the pros. Courage is therefore a highly relative concept that can only apply to other people's feats.

creativity   Process by which new ideas are produced. This can be done by individuals or teams. It can be enhanced or blocked by the value system that exists in the environment.

creed   A fourth, but optional, layer of our knowledge. Creed relates our understanding of the world to a transcendent, supernatural, ultimate reference. Creed can either totally replace the wisdom layer of our knowledge, by providing a specific set of answers concerning the meaning of the world, or come in addition to our philosophical understanding of things, relating it in turn to an ultimate reference that lies beyond this world. Creed, however, is not the result of experience or of rational deduction but of an act of faith.

desires One of the forms of our emotions, the other being our impressions. Our desires result from our impressions, and represent our reaction to what our impressions have told us about the state of accomplishment of our PTL. Our desires lead to actions that we will take to change our Power-to-Live in a way that it becomes always more favourable to our PTL.

drama We call *dramatic* the consequences of an event that have a negative impact on our PTL. This qualification we oppose to the one of *tragic*, which we apply to any situation when we need to make a decision that might have favourable or dramatic results for us. Life is tragic because it forces us to constantly make choices that will lead one way or the other to more or less dramatic outcomes, in the sense that they will negatively impact our Power-to-Live.

emotions One of the three dimensions of our Way-to-Live, the others being actions and rest. Our emotions are either the signals that our PTL sends back to itself to inform us of the state of its accomplishment (we call these impressions) or the reactions that we develop to such impressions, which take the form of a resulting need to act upon our Power-to-Live (we call these desires).

energy Another way of expressing our Vitality Quotient. It reflects the degree to which we tend to mobilise our vital functions in order to accomplish our PTL. Our energy is the most basic form of our Power-to-Live, the element that allows all the other categories of our power to materialise and become effective. Energy is in a sense the fuel of life.

entertainment

The form of action by which we tend to stimulate our vital functions for the mere purpose of this stimulation itself. Contrary to work, entertainment does not aim at an output that will preserve or enhance our Power-to-Live, but only at the mobilisation of our functions in order to intensify our impression of living. The pleasure of entertainment comes from this intensification itself. One must remain aware, however, that entertainment is but an illusion of life and not the actual implementation of our PTL

equation of life

A formula which allows us to measure the value for us of an action. This equation includes three factors: the *output* of the action in terms of enhancement of our Power-to-Live, the *degree* to which it stimulates our vital functions and finally its *cost* in terms of Power-to-Live that we have already acquired. When the equation of life is positive, we decide to proceed with the contemplated action; when it's negative we refrain and prefer to turn to another alternative.

ethics

A code of behaviour that is meant to benefit our PTL by providing the best possible rules of conduct when we are faced with a given situation. A tool meant to serve us, and not the opposite. Ethics should be challenged in relation to their purpose and revised when appropriate. We have our own ethical code.

freedom

The only freedom we may or may not have, according to our model, is the freedom of movement, of doing what we want and can do. But we are not free to decide what we want to do or will do. This is determined by our Will-to-Live which defines our basic driving need, and our Power-to-Live which fixes the means we have to do something, including our ability to choose what thing to do. Our lack of free will, however, does not absolve us of our responsibility for what we eventually decide to do.

imagination   The individual capacity to visualise something that does not yet exist.

impressions   One of our two forms of emotions, the other being our desires. Impressions tell us the state of accomplishment of our PTL. Good impressions signify that we are in good shape, bad impressions indicate a threat to our PTL. Impressions can be immediate (sensations) or related to an anticipated effect of a thing on our PTL (feelings).

immorality   An attitude by which we infringe our code of ethics. This can be either a good or a bad thing for our PTL. It is bad if we transgress a command of our ethical code that we still consider valid, but which at this very moment we do not feel as pressing as the immediate advantage expected from the immoral action that we contemplate. By going for this short-term advantage, we will give ourselves an immediate pleasure but will end up regretting the longer-term cost to our PTL of the choice that we made. It is good, on the other hand, when the transgression reflects our judgement that our code of ethics is no longer appropriate to serve our PTL and needs to be revised.

information   The second layer of our knowledge. Information relates the notions contained in our scientific understanding of the world to us personally, i.e. to our intentions, desires and wills. Something becomes meaningful for us, as living beings, as soon as we can refer it to a purpose that we have.

innovation   The translation of invention into deeds as well as into socially acceptable new norms.

knowledge   Our representation of the world, i.e. of everything that is. We also refer to knowledge as our idea of the world and of our existence. Knowledge is structured according to the use we make of it. The main elements of this structure are: science, information, wisdom and possibly creed.

leadership   The process by which some people mobilise others around a vision or a cause. It is about change and getting results. It can also be defined (in the corporate world) as the ability to give a chance to people to perform, enjoy and grow in the job. It is also about inventing tomorrow today, making the difference, and even better seeing what others do not see.

life   Life has the form of a project, the Project-to-Live. To live is to want to live. Life has no other aim than its own perpetuation. All living beings have this same form and purpose. Our life, our existence and our PTL mean the same thing.

mind   One of our vital capacities, by which the PTL is able to represent itself in all its dimensions and thus act in the best interests of its own accomplishment. By our mind we will imply both our physiological organs, which allow us to think, and the thinking process itself.

morals   Morals are part of our ethics. They refer to the code of conduct that we adopt towards others. Our moral conduct is based mainly on self-interest, but we recognise that we are also capable of doing totally disinterested things in favour of other people; when this happens, we attribute it to the fact that we tend to identify with our fellow humans and by a sheer effect of our imagination will sometimes value their PTL as if it were our own and treat it as such.

ownership

The attitude of those who recognise that once they are projected in this world as PTLs, they are fully in charge of their destiny. Taking ownership implies that one doesn't turn to other authorities to beg for assistance or to complain, and that one is in charge of one's own code of conduct (ethics) so as to optimise one's behaviour. Ownership is another word for *responsibility*.

philosophy

A word that has multiple meanings, which all more or less relate to the understanding and value that we attribute to the world around us, to life and everything that those notions comprise. Also extends to how we deal or should deal with things, i.e. the actual practice of our existence.

In this book, philosophy is essentially understood as the overall meaning and purpose we give to the world and to our life, the two being intricately meshed.

Power-to-Live

The second module of the structure of our PTL. It is the means by which we can carry on with and accomplish our PTL. Our Power-to-Live is made of all the elements of the world, and the specific disposition according to which they converge towards our own personal PTL: 'I am the world.' We are all different in the way that our Power-to-Live is composed.

Power Map

Our individual Power Map reflects the composition of our Power-to-Live. It includes the categories of Power-to-Live that we rely on preferably to ensure the accomplishment of our PTL. We are all different in the way that we build up and make use of our Power Maps. To understand someone's Power Map is to get to know the identity and idiosyncrasies of that person and therefore to learn how to deal with her in the best way.

predetermination   Means the fact that we are not 'free' to want something or not to want it, nor to decide in one way rather than the other. We are not free to want because we are born as a Will-to-Live, so that our fundamental desire is inscribed in us from the beginning and throughout our entire existence. All our other desires will derive from this initial need that we do not control. Nor are we free to act in one way rather than the other, because all our actions emanate from our Power-to-Live as it is given at every instant. We can only decide by taking into account all the contents of our Power-to-Live which already exists, and therefore we really have no real choice one way or the other.

PTL   The name of our model and the ultimate reference of meaning of our understanding of the world. The Project-to-Live is the concept by which we define our being and the form of our existence in this world. We are nothing else than a project, the project of our own perpetuation. Our PTL is structured according to three elements: the Will-to-Live, the Power-to-Live, the Way-to-Live.

reference   The stepping stone to knowledge. In order to know something we need to refer it to something else, which we have already integrated into our knowledge, and that we call the reference. In the basic phrases that lead to our knowledge, 'This is that' or 'This results from that', 'that' is the reference. When we think 'philosophically', we search for an ultimate reference to which we can relate everything that composes our world and which will thus give a meaning to it all. In our case here, the ultimate reference is the PTL.

responsibility The notion that we are accountable for everything that we do in life. In the framework of the PTL model, accountability is basically and ultimately to ourselves, to our Will-to-Live. Even if we have no freedom to decide what we are to do, we will nevertheless have to bear the consequences of our acts, good or bad. The paradox lies in the fact that we are responsible while not free to decide upon what we do.

rest One of the forms of our Way-to-Live, by which our vital functions are in a state of regeneration. In fact, rest is a way of speech: we never really rest since when we demobilise one or the other of our organs or limbs for it to regenerate, we expect another function to switch on that will move to accomplish the regeneration process. Rest is therefore a way of distracting a vital capacity from its productive purpose in order to switch it over to a temporary regeneration mode. Total rest would imply the end of our PTL ('Rest in peace...').

science The first layer of knowledge. Science is a network of meanings, in which each element relates to one or several other elements, while all these elements (things that compose the world) can individually become a reference of meaning for the others. In science, no particular element plays the role of ultimate reference of meaning.

tragedy The tragic dimension of our existence lies in the fact that we constantly need to make decisions which engage our PTL. We can never know in advance what the consequences of such choices will be, and in

271

themselves they always imply that we renounce one possible way (make a sacrifice) in favour of another. Therefore all our decisions have a cost in terms of our Power-to-Live, and this cost means a reduction of this power, thus a weakening of our PTL, which of course we hope and expect to overcompensate by the positive outcome of the decision made.

selfishness

The natural characteristic of any human being, whose first obligation is to ensure his or her own perpetuation. Selfishness is the necessary basic attitude that keeps us alive, i.e. in conformity with our PTL. When we transcend selfishness to become altruistic, it is only because we understand that we have more to gain by doing so, so that altruism becomes another way of being selfish. Even when we carry out totally disinterested acts, we behave that way because we identify through our imagination with the person we serve, and treat him/her as if it were our own PTL that we were preserving.

self-sacrifice

A form of suicide (although self-sacrifice does not always lead to death!) by which we seem to go against the principle of the PTL and do things that don't actually lead to the perpetuation of our own existence. This is however only a false impression, for self-sacrifice is also in its way a means of accomplishing our own PTL, either because we expect from such a deed some beneficial return in this or the next world, or because we identify so strongly with the person we sacrifice to, that by satisfying his or her needs we feel that we are indeed satisfying those of our own PTL.

suicide

This is an act which can at first sight appear as a negation of the essence of the Project-to-Live model, since it seems to imply that there is at least one instance where human beings will decide to go against their very essence, which is their will to perpetuate their existence. We have demonstrated, however, that this is not the case and that suicide is actually a paradoxical and extreme situation which, when analysed carefully, confirms that here as ever we tend towards nothing less than the ultimate satisfaction of our Will-to-Live.

truth

Truth is no more than the validity that we attribute to our own representation of the world (our knowledge) at any given moment in time. We consider that the way we see the world is true, until our perceptions lead us to see it differently. Our personal view of the world is thus always necessarily true, until proven otherwise to us. We will therefore consider that a representation of things that differs from our own is not true (although acceptable, of course, if we are tolerant of others). Our 'truth' varies constantly, as we adjust our understanding of the world at every instant.

value

The value we attribute to something completes our understanding (knowledge) of that thing, in so far as it indicates to what degree that thing will impact our PTL in a positive or negative fashion. Unless we give value to things we can not determine how to act towards them. Our knowledge is complete only when it includes our *evaluation* of what we know.

vital functions

All the parts that constitute our living organism and which jointly contribute to the perpetuation of our PTL. We constantly mobilise our vital functions to accomplish our PTL, either consciously or through reflex activities. The stimulations of our vital functions are conducive to an impression of pleasure, since they reflect an active dedication on our part to the accomplishment of our PTL. Conversely, when we do not mobilise our vital functions, and leave them idle, we rapidly feel a negative impression which we call boredom, and which tells us that we are not devoting ourselves sufficiently to our purpose, which is to implement our PTL.

Way-to-Live   The third module of the structure of our PTL. It is everything that we do and feel. It describes our actual existence. Our Way-to-Live is the activation of our Power-to-Live. Since we all have a different Power-to-Live, we also all behave differently in the way that we carry out our existence (see *behaviour*).

Will-to-Live   The first module of the structure of the PTL. The Will-to-Live is the essence of the PTL and of our very being. The Will-to-Live is what all living beings have in common. We are all identical in that we have as a basic drive our will to perpetuate our existence.

wisdom   The third layer of our knowledge. Wisdom is the result of our science and information being connected to an ultimate reference of meaning which gives sense to the whole. Wisdom allows us to make sense of the world in general as well as of our existence, and to order our behaviour accordingly. Wisdom is another word for philosophy as we have understood it here, although one could also say that philosophy encompasses all our knowledge, including the two other layers mentioned before.

work   One of the two forms of action, the other being entertainment. By our work we strive to preserve and/or enhance our Power-to-Live. Work is thus a condition of life, to the extent that we may say, 'To live is to work and to work is to live.'

Further reading

The following list is a very short selection of some of the authors' favourite books on the topics addressed in this work. Obviously, any reader interested in philosophy, or in any other of the subjects discussed in our book, should do his or her own research (try Google...) to go deeper.

Philosophy

A History of Western Philosophy, Bertrand Russell
The Oxford Companion to Philosophy
Confessions of a Philosopher, Brian Magee
The Fountainhead, Ayn Rand
The Open Society and its Enemies, Karl Popper

Business

Winning, J Welch
Shift, C Ghosn
Who says elephants cannot dance?, L Gerstner
Good to Great, J Collins
Confronting Reality, L Bossidy and R Charan

Leadership

Leading Change, J Kotter
Authentic Leadership, B George
Philosophy in Action, P Claudel and P Casse
Leading the Revolution, G Hamel
Virtuoso Teams, A Boynton and B Fischer

The World

The World is Flat, T Friedman
The Wealth and Poverty of Nations, D Landes
Post-Capitalist Society, P Drucker
Guns, Germs and Steel, J Diamond
The Roaring Nineties, J E Stiglitz

Creativity

Disruption, J-M Dru
Blink, M Gladwell
Provocative Therapy, F Farrelly and J Brandsma
Lateral Thinking, Edward de Bono
Mind Mapping, T Buzan

Printed in the United States
94092LV00004B/43-126/A